THE PRESENT ECONOMIC REVOLUTION IN THE UNITED STATES

By Thomas Nixon Carver

THE DISTRIBUTION OF WEALTH

PRINCIPLES OF RURAL ECONOMICS

ESSAYS IN SOCIAL JUSTICE

PRINCIPLES OF NATIONAL ECONOMY

THE ECONOMY OF HUMAN ENERGY

THE PRESENT ECONOMIC REVOLUTION

IN THE UNITED STATES

By

THOMAS NIXON CARVER

Professor of Political Economy, Harvard University

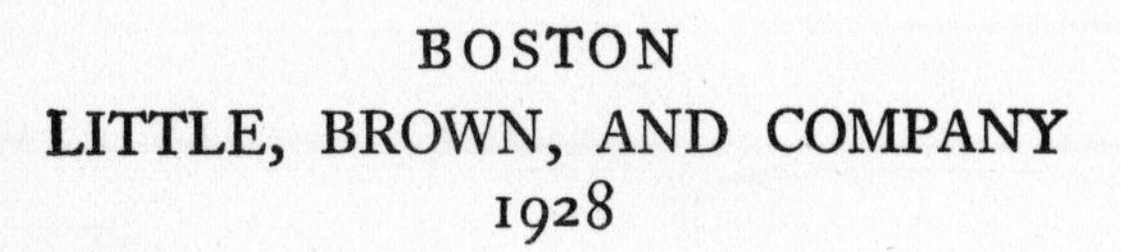

BOSTON

LITTLE, BROWN, AND COMPANY

1928

Printed in the United States of America

TO THOSE STEADY MINDS

THAT HAVE NEVER LOST THEIR FAITH IN THE POSSIBILITY OF EQUALITY UNDER LIBERTY, NOR BEEN WILLING TO ACCEPT EQUALITY WITHOUT LIBERTY, NOR LIBERTY WITHOUT EQUALITY, AS THE FINAL GOAL OF DEMOCRACY

FOREWORD

THE economic changes now occurring in the United States are significant in their relation to the whole history of Western Civilization — as significant perhaps as the Industrial Revolution in England at the close of the eighteenth century.

It is not mere chance that this present revolution is taking place in the United States before it begins anywhere else. Our stage was set for it in 1888. We were then the youthful giant in industry. We had just grown out of our infancy into young nationhood. We were a tireless producing nation with fabulous accumulations of wealth and with almost incalculable resources still to draw upon. Even more important than our natural resources were our democratic traditions that gave every man a fair chance, that placed no handicaps upon success, that permitted every one to rise as high in business, in profession, and in politics, as his abilities would justify. Our immense industrial population was earning more in purchasing power than the industrialists of any other country.

During the next thirty years this economic prosperity was not only maintained, but the discrepancy between earnings abroad and in the United States even increased, so that in the second quarter of the twentieth century, our people find themselves amazingly better off than those of other lands. Notably, because of the stoppage of immigration by the war, followed by restrictive legislation, our wage workers have continued to earn a larger share in this prosperity than wage workers have ever gained. What is the result? It is a change in social and economic conditions undreamed of even by our leaders of a single generation back.

This major movement in the development of our American national life is described by Professor Carver. As the third of the books on American nationalism it emphasizes certain constructive forces, and brings into high relief what are perhaps the most hopeful tendencies of modern industrial society.

HENRY BASS HALL,
General Editor.

CONTENTS

THE PRESENT ECONOMIC REVOLUTION IN THE UNITED STATES

CHAPTER ONE

Introductory

I

FORTY years or more ago, it began to be fashionable to comment, on the one hand, upon the awful concentration of wealth in this country, and, on the other, upon the masses of poverty that were concentrated in the slums of our cities. A flood of ink was poured upon the subject, and lecturers made the ears of the public to tingle with horror at the evils of the so-called capitalist system. Some went so far as to say not only that the rich were growing richer and the poor poorer, but that this was the inevitable result of the capitalist system. Plutocracy and poverty were its twin offspring. The public was asked to choose between capitalism with its hideous progeny and some other system, say socialism, with all its difficulties. We were told positively that we had no other choice; that the modern world was between the devil of plutocracy and the deep sea of socialism.

In all of this discussion the facts were perverted and the underlying principles misstated, and yet there were certain large and visible facts that lent a semblance of color to the argument. If any one undertook to show that such results were not necessary products of the present economic system, the huge fortunes of our multimillionaires and the slums of our cities were pointed out to him as evidence to the contrary. Here was something that was difficult to explain; at least to the satisfaction of minds that were not trained to clear economic analysis.

The speeches that were written during the period from 1870 to 1910 are now out of date, and yet a considerable number of people who learned their speeches then are unable to stop. They are still repeating them with parrot-like persistency. Instead of the concentration of wealth, we are now witnessing its diffusion; but the old tirades against plutocracy are still repeated. Instead of low wages for the manual trades, we are now having high wages; and yet the old phraseology, including such terms as wage slavery, still has a certain vogue. Instead of the laborer being in a position of dependence, he is now rapidly attaining a position of independence. The apostles of discontent are being robbed of their thunder. Some of them are even showing signs of resentment toward the present tendency to improve the condition of labor because it has robbed them of a pet grievance.

To the economic mind it was apparent, even in that period of labor depression, that the enormous differences in wealth and prosperity which then came to different classes were not a necessary result of the capitalist system; that it is just as possible to attain equality under capitalism as under any other system; that the inequalities which exist under it are due to disturbing factors that are easily removable and are not due to the nature of the system itself.

On the other hand, untrained minds were asserting that the capitalist system was about to collapse; that it was inherently bad and could not endure. As a matter of fact, capitalism could no more collapse than peace could collapse or liberty collapse. Peace cannot collapse; it can be destroyed by force, and nothing but force can destroy it. Liberty cannot collapse; it can likewise be destroyed by force, and nothing but force can destroy it. In the absence of force, peace and liberty simply exist; they do not have to be created or supported. Capitalism has its beginnings in a condition under which no man can be dispossessed of what he has produced or discovered except with his own consent. In the absence of force, capitalism automatically exists in the same sense that peace and liberty automatically exist. That is to say, if the man who has made a tool cannot be dispossessed of it without his consent, it is his. If he is dispossessed with his consent, that is, if he sells it to somebody else, then that other person cannot be dispossessed without his own consent; he owns the tool. Whether the tool be a small one or a large one, the same principle applies. You cannot destroy capitalism until you make it possible for the producer to be dispossessed of his product against his consent. That implies the use of force. To talk about capitalism collapsing is, therefore, to be devoid of understanding.

The time has come when it is no longer necessary to rely upon theoretical analysis to show that wealth can be diffused under the system of voluntary agreement. Prosperity can be given to all classes, without giving up the system of voluntary agreement among free citizens as the method of getting things done. We are actually beginning to achieve a wider diffusion of prosperity; students know it, and everybody else feels it, except those few who are still harping on the old theme.

To have said this forty years ago or even twenty years ago would have been unconvincing to any except the more analytical students of economics. Those who said it were like voices crying in the wilderness. We now have facts enough on our side to convince any except the most stubborn apostles of discontent. One of the purposes of this book is to convince reasonable minds that it is not only possible to have a wide diffusion of prosperity among all classes, but that we are actually beginning to realize that possibility here and now.

The world, however, will not be robbed of all its grievances. Now that wages are high and likely, sooner or later, to go higher, another class of pessimists is beginning to wonder whether civilization can maintain itself or not. How can we have servants to do our rough work for us if they insist on having wages that are comparable with the incomes of the heads of our households? How can we possibly build the new enterprises that civilization demands unless we have cheap labor? How can we entertain graciously unless we can have an hereditary servant class to relieve the hostess of all responsibility? What is to become of the old benevolent and paternal relationship between employer and employee, if employees insist on making of their labor a commodity and selling it to the highest bidder? In those countries where there is a chronic oversupply of labor, labor is never a commodity; it accepts the condition of dependence, attaches itself to some patron, and insists on a paternal relationship. Almost without exception, as soon as labor begins to be scarce and hard to find, laborers insist on breaking up this old personal relationship and treating their own labor as a commodity, selling it in the highest market. Thus it happens that, in the most economically advanced countries, labor itself insists, in practice if not in words, that labor is a commodity. Those who regret the old, paternal relationship and long for a condition in which laborers are dependents are, of course, pessimistic regarding the new situation and wonder whether civilization can endure or not. Another purpose of this book is to show that the conditions that make labor a commodity tend toward a higher state of civilization than the conditions that make it a dependency.

II

The Great War produced a number of political revolutions in Europe. It has not yet produced an economic revolution.[1] A number of old governments have been overthrown and new ones set up in their places. In some cases this resulted in a temporary economic debacle, but wherever industry has begun to function again it looks so much like that which existed before the revolution as to be difficult to distinguish from it. No significant improvement over the old forms of industry has yet been produced in any European country by any of these political revolutions. Their ultimate economic effects go no deeper than those that follow the ousting of one gang of politicians from the government of an American city and the substitution of another.

An economic revolution may follow as a result of a political revolution, but usually it does not. According to De Tocqueville the one significant economic result of the French Revolution, which was primarily political, was that the land of the peasants was freed from a multitude of duties and restrictions and became their property in a more complete sense

[1] *See* an article by the writer in *Aera*, also in the *Electric Railway Journal*, October, 1924.

than it had ever been.[1] Up to the present (1925) that is the only economic improvement over the old régime that is noticeable in Russia; yet the specific purpose of the Russian revolutionists was to use the power of government to force a new economic order upon the people. In spite of the most ruthless exercise of governmental power which the modern world has ever seen, they have found the economic forces too much for them. As to the peasants and the land, the most that the revolution did was to accelerate a process that was already going on. More than that, the whole process was toward the private ownership of land, which is the direct antithesis of communism. In short, the economic forces brought about the private ownership of land by the peasants in spite of rather than with the help of the new political power with its communistic notions.

Economic revolutions usually proceed from causes that lie deeper than politics or government. The most that a government can do is to hasten or retard them, and even this is not always possible.

The only economic revolution now under way is going on in the United States. It is a revolution that is to wipe out the distinction between laborers and capitalists by making laborers their own capitalists and by compelling most capitalists to become laborers of one kind or another, because not many

[1] *See* Alexis de Tocqueville: "The Old Régime and the Revolution." Harper & Brothers, New York, 1856. Translated by John Bonner.

of them will be able to live on the returns from capital alone. This is something new in the history of the world.

The labor movement in this country is so far in advance of that in any other country as to make comparison impossible. In European countries, including Great Britain, labor organizations and the more conspicuous labor leaders are still pursuing antiquated methods that are comparable to the attempt of a man to lift himself by his boot straps. Here they are using the solid ground of capital ownership and are actually lifting themselves into positions of well-being that amount to affluence in comparison with the conditions of European laborers. In European countries their organized, political activities are dominated by a psychology that was built up in a primitive and fighting stage of social development; here they are emerging from that stage and are beginning to think in constructive terms such as belong to a progressive and industrial stage. In European countries they are grasping at the shadow of political control, but never have and never will by that method put an ounce of the substance of economic prosperity into the hands of any laborer. In this country they have, with few exceptions, refused to be deceived by shadows and are rapidly gaining the real substance of prosperity.

Those minds that are still thinking in terms of the primitive tactics of class war will not understand a single syllable of the last paragraph. The labor movement in this country is passing out of the stage in which leadership concerned itself mainly with the immediate tactics of battle. It is passing into the stage where it is concerning itself with the higher strategy of labor. This higher strategy takes account of the permanent economic forces and puts laborers in a position where these forces work for them rather than against them. Instead of continuing to fight capital they are beginning to recognize its power and to use it as an implement for their own improvement. There are at least three kinds of evidence that indicate roughly the extent to which laborers are becoming their own capitalists: first, the rapid growth of savings deposits; second, the investment by laborers in the shares of corporations; third, the growth of labor banks. These will be discussed in later chapters.

These improvements will inevitably produce a change in the so-called relationship between capital and labor. This does not mean that every possible source of conflict between employers and employees will be removed. Such a possibility does not exist. "Every possible human relationship has in it elements of conflict as well as elements of harmony. This is true of the most intimate and the tenderest of human relations, as well as of the most perfunctory and businesslike. Even husband and wife, if they permit themselves to think of such things, will find elements of conflict in such questions as the division of the income, who shall have the auto on a given afternoon, etc. Their relationship also, of course, has many elements of harmony. Each needs the other, and in a great multitude of ways each gains in proportion as the other gains. Whether they live in peace and harmony or in a state of antagonism depends upon which aspect of their relationship they permit themselves to think about most frequently. If they permit themselves to forget their need of one another and the many questions on which their interests harmonize, and to think only of the questions on which there is a conflict of interest, they are not likely to live a very harmonious life. But if, on the other hand, those questions on which there is a unity of interests occupy their minds, they may expect nothing but peace and harmony.

"Even the most perfunctory and businesslike relationship also has its elements of harmony. The producer, for example, needs the consumer, and the consumer needs the producer. When consumers are prosperous, they make better customers for the producer. When producers are prosperous, they are likely to be stimulated to higher endeavor in the service of consumers. On the other hand, when they meet face to face, to bargain over prices, they find a very definite source of conflict. The producer would like to sell at a higher price; the consumer would like to buy at a lower price, and there may be a great deal of 'higgling the market.' If they forget their need of one another and the large elements of harmony in their relationship, and think of nothing except the immediate problem of bargaining and the irritation that grows out of it, there may grow up a mutual hostility which, when shared in by large numbers, may result in the injury of both classes. The same may be repeated with respect to employer and employee, capitalist and laborer, student and teacher, parent and child."[1]

While the economic changes that are now in progress will not eliminate every possible source of conflict between employers and employees, they will produce a change in the state of mind toward things about which employers and employees habitually think. Laborers who are themselves capitalists in a small way will be compelled by that circumstance to think somewhat more about capital. They will understand a little more clearly what it is and what it does. Employers likewise who find it necessary to work harder than before, in order to make anything out of their capital, will be compelled to think a little more about the problems of their employees, and both employer and employee will be compelled to think more about the common enterprise in which they are engaged, from which each derives his income, and on whose growth and prosperity the wel-

[1] *See* Carver and Hall, "Human Relations", D. C. Heath & Company, 1923, Chapter XVII.

fare of both classes depends. This in itself should bring a greater degree of harmony between them, as surely as a greater degree of harmony comes to husband and wife when they think primarily of the things that unite them rather than of the things that divide them; or when producer and consumer think of their common interests rather than of their antagonisms. This will be a new thing in the modern world; and we are justified in calling it an economic revolution.

CHAPTER TWO

AN AMERICAN IDEAL

I

A YEAR or so ago a popular bishop was quoted as saying that Russia was the only country in the world that was pursuing an ideal. That would be startling, if true, but it must be classed among those statements that are designed to attract attention rather than to convey accurate information. The Bolsheviki are followers of Karl Marx and their experiment was based upon his teachings. If there is anything that Marx and his followers are unanimous in repudiating, it is idealism of every kind. They make a sharp distinction between what they call Utopian and scientific socialism. That distinction is simply that Utopian socialism is idealistic, and Marxian or scientific socialism is materialistic and strictly self-interested. Marx and his followers have taught the proletarians to shun all ideals as devices of the ruling classes to hold the masses in subjection, and to look after themselves alone.

One of their leading doctrines is the materialistic interpretation of history which, under Marx's perversion, allows for no idealism of any kind. This doctrine in its more scientific form did not originate with

Marx, nor was he its most erudite and logical expounder. Buckle did it much better. Marx combined it, however, with another doctrine, that of evolution through class struggle. These two doctrines in combination leave no room for any form of idealism. Neither doctrine, taken alone, is so very deadly; at least, no more so than any other false doctrine. In combination, however, they are perfectly deadly and completely destructive, not only of our material civilization, but of all the ideals on which any civilization was ever based. The present revolution in Russia is a proletarian revolution, based on the crass self-interest of the so-called proletarians. They do not even profess to be working for ideals. They profess to be working for their own material self-interest. They do not stand for ideals; they stand for themselves alone. In this they are consistent followers of the teachings of Marx.

A consistent disciple of Marx, Mr. Charles H. Kerr, published, sometime ago, a little pamphlet entitled "The Folly of Being 'Good.'" [1] It begins with a Platonic dialogue.

"'But,' my friend asks, 'do you mean to say that it is wise to be bad?'

"That depends. Who is to decide what is good and what is bad?

"I will tell you who does decide. It is John D. Rockefeller.

[1] Published by Charles H. Kerr and Company, Chicago.

"I use his name because it may help to make clear a rather abstract statement which will express the same idea more scientifically. The prevailing moral ideas among masses of people are the result of the conditions under which the people have supplied themselves and are supplying themselves with their food and the other necessities of life. And in a society like that in America to-day, where there is a ruling class, like the capitalists, and subject class, like the laborers, the moral ideas are such as will, if followed out generally, be best for the interests of the ruling class.

"The word 'good' has had many meanings, it has many meanings still, according to the connection in which it is used, and when I speak of the folly of being 'good', I mean 'good' in the sense in which it is used by the teachers, preachers, editors and writers who are, consciously or unconsciously, working for the interests of Mr. Rockefeller and his class."

This quotation may sound somewhat mysterious to one who is not versed in the teachings of Marx. To one who is familiar with Marx it is perfectly clear and is what could be expected of any of his followers. One who has not studied the teachings of Marx and of his followers does not understand the first thing that has happened in Russia during or since the revolution. It is perfectly clear to any one who has read Marx understandingly, and it is the logical teaching of one who accepts the two Marxian doctrines — the materialistic interpretation of history and the doctrine of evolution through class struggle — and who also understands that the Bolsheviki believe those doctrines.

According to this teaching there is, to begin with, no God. What is more to the point, there is no such thing as right and wrong in any positive sense. Right and wrong are mere conventional ideas. Whatever happens to be approved by the people of a given time and place is for them right; what they disapprove is wrong. There is no higher court of appeal; there is no other test. If it is generally agreed that lying, stealing, and rape are commendable, they are commendable. If it is generally agreed that they are not commendable, they are not; that is all there is to it.

When Marx's materialistic interpretation of history is combined with the doctrine of evolution through class struggle, it becomes even more strange to Christian ears.

According to this, our conventional notions of right and wrong are determined for us at any time and place by the dominant class. When the fighting class was dominant, their ideas prevailed; what they said was right, became right; what they said was wrong, became wrong. When the priests dominated, they determined right and wrong for us. If they said that a given thing was right, it became right; if they said that a given thing was wrong, it became wrong. Everybody followed their example, approved what they said was right, and disapproved what they said was wrong. At other times and places the capitalist class is dominant. If they say that a given thing is right, it becomes right; if they say that it is wrong, it becomes wrong. The rest of us are led to approve what they say is right and to disapprove what they say is wrong. That is what Mr. Kerr meant to imply very specifically when he affirmed that Mr. Rockefeller determined what was right and what was wrong in this country at the present time.

In all these cases the class that is in a position of domination and which, because of this position, determines for us what is right and wrong, always decides in its own interest. When the priests dominated the ideas of society, they made everybody believe that it was right to do what the priestly class found it to their interest to have the people do. It was right to pay tithes because it was profitable to the priestly class that people should pay tithes. It was right to revere God or the gods because this gave the priestly class power over people through its interpretation of the will of God or of the gods. And so the whole moral system was planned for the profit of the priestly class. When the capitalist class became dominant and was in a position to determine what was right and what was wrong, and make the rest of us believe it, they invariably made us believe that it was right to do whatever was profitable for the capitalist. It is right to be industrious because it is profitable to the capitalist that we should be industrious. It is right to be honest because it is profitable to the capitalist class that we should be honest. It is right, especially, to respect property and not steal because it is profitable to the capitalist class that we should respect property and not steal it; and so on. The whole moral system was built up by capitalists in the interest of capitalists.

"From this point of view," says Engels, Marx's chief disciple and interpreter, "the final causes of all social changes and political revolutions are to be sought, not in men's brains, not in man's better insight into eternal truth and justice, but in changes in the modes of production and exchange."[1]

Again, he says, "The merchant or manufacturer himself stood in the position of master, or, as it was until lately called, of 'natural superior' to his clerks, his workpeople, his domestic servants. His interest was to get as much and as good work out of them as he could; for this end they had to be trained to proper submission. He was himself religious; his religion had supplied the standard under which he had fought the king and the lords; he was not long in discovering the opportunities this same religion offered him for working upon the minds of his natural

[1] "Socialism, Utopian and Scientific", by Friedrich Engels. Translated by Edward Aveling. Page 45. London, S. Sonnenschien and Company. New York, Charles Scribner's Sons, 1892.

inferiors, making them submissive to the behests of the masters it had pleased God to put over them. In short, the English bourgeoisie now had to take a part in keeping down the 'lower orders', the great producing mass of the nation, and one of the means employed for that purpose was the influence of religion."[1]

Speaking of the revolutionary uprisings of 1848 on the Continent, Engels says:

"If the British bourgeois had been convinced before of the necessity of maintaining the common people in a religious mood, how much more must he feel that necessity after all these experiences? Regardless of the sneers of his Continental compeers, he continued to spend thousands and tens of thousands, year after year, upon the evangelism of the lower orders; not content with his own native religious machinery, he appealed to Brother Jonathan, the greatest organizer in existence of religion as a trade, and imported from America revivalism, Moody and Sankey, and the like; and, finally, he accepted the dangerous aid of the Salvation Army, which revives the propaganda of early Christianity, appeals to the poor as the elect, fights capitalism in a religious way, and thus fosters an element of early Christian class antagonism, which one day may become troublesome to the well-to-do people who now find the ready money for it."[2]

The next stage, according to the Marxian teaching, is that in which the proletarians become domi-

[1] *Op. cit.*, introduction, page xxv. [2] *Op. cit.*, introduction, page xxxi.

nant and are in a position to determine what is right and what is wrong. They do not profess to be seeking right or justice except in a purely conventional sense, because according to their materialistic interpretation, there is no such thing as right and justice except in a purely conventional sense. They are going to tell us what is right and what is wrong and force us to accept it; but what is right under this new régime will be what is profitable to the proletarians. What is wrong will be what is unprofitable to the proletarians. It is conceived, for example, to be against the interest of the proletarians that any one should call anything his own. Therefore they will make it wrong for any one to call anything his own. If any one does call anything his own, it will be to the interest of the proletarians for some one to dispossess him or take it away from him; therefore they will make it right to dispossess the one who pretends to any form of ownership. Again, there is no idealism about this; it is believed, however mistakenly, to be for the purely material gain of the dominant class which, under the revolution, is the proletarian class. There is no more idealism about this than there was when the capitalists made us believe that what was profitable to them was right and what was unprofitable was wrong.

If you ask a thorough-going follower of Marx whether he thinks it is right to do some of the things that the Bolsheviki have done, you will not disturb him in the least. He will merely ask, "What do you mean by right? Who determines what is right and what is wrong? In Russia the Bolsheviki are going to determine what is right and what is wrong. If they decide that it is to their interest to do what they are doing, that makes it right." If any one doubts this, let him read Trotsky's "The Defence of Terrorism."[1] This is the kind of idealism which our popular bishop apparently approves, if we are permitted to interpret his language intelligently.

The Marxian socialists' general opposition to international war is sometimes accounted to them for righteousness. Possibly this is what the bishop had in mind when he spoke of the idealism of the Bolsheviki. The so-called pacifism of the Marxian socialist, however, is not based on any fundamental opposition to war. He is only opposed to war between those territorial groups called States or Nations. He advocates war between those non-territorial groups called classes. The advocate of class war is no more of an idealist than the advocate of international war.

There are some pacifists who, like Tolstoi, are opposed to war of any sort; who are not opposed to government as such, but to all exercise of force; who are not opposed to nationalism as such, but are only opposed to nationalism when it eventuates in war. Such a pacifist is just as opposed to class

[1] The Labour Publishing Company, Ltd. London, 1921.

war as to international war, and to the use of force to resist government as to the use of force in support of government. There is, undoubtedly, a kind of idealism about this, even though it is utterly irrational and impracticable; but this kind of idealistic pacifism ought never to be confused with the materialistic, class-conscious pacifism of the Marxian socialist who denounces international war in one breath and preaches class war in the next. Such spurious pacifism is more likely to be based on cowardice than on idealism.

As the ultimate outcome of the war of the classes, it is contended that peace will be established through the elimination of all classes except one. When the entire population is included in one class, namely, the proletariat, there can obviously be no longer any war of the classes. This argument runs parallel to one that has always been in the minds of military imperialists from Cæsar down to Napoleon and the ex-Kaiser. If all other nations of the earth could be conquered by one nation and brought under one great empire, there would be no such thing as international wars any more because there would be no nations left to fight among themselves. The *pax Romana* was a real thing while it lasted.

Unfortunately, this reasoning overlooks the possibility of civil war. When the whole world was under the Roman Empire, of course there could be no war between the Roman Empire and any other; but civil war was not only a possibility, it became an actuality, and civil wars are quite as bitter and destructive as international wars. A similar idea was apparently in the minds of the German militarists before the Great War. If the Kaiser could be made a sort of super-Kaiser, ruling over the entire world, of course there could be no such thing as international war any longer. This was a plausible line of reasoning which led to the conclusion that through militarism world peace would be established. The German militarists could therefore with straight faces pose as apostles of peace. They were apostles of peace in the same sense that the Bolsheviki are.

Their reasoning, of course, overlooked the fact that it might be difficult to hold a great empire together and avoid civil war. The *pax Germanica* might have been a real thing, while it lasted, though the process of achieving it might be somewhat painful. Again, the process of breaking such a world empire up again into a number of territorial units would also be painful.

If the Bolsheviki could exterminate or eliminate all other classes and leave only the proletarians, there could, of course, no longer be a war between classes — at least that might be true for a time. The *pax Bolshevika* might be a real thing while it lasted, but one who believes that there is no conflict but only harmony of interests among all proletarians must be rather naïve.

Wherever a conflict of interests exists there is at least the possibility of strife and even of war. It all depends on how willing each group is to surrender some advantage in the interest of peace. If the love of peace is very strong, and the desire to promote its own interest not very strong, peace would be certain among the various groups, occupational and otherwise, that make up the proletariat. If the desire for self-interest is very strong, and the love of peace not so strong, war would be certain. The history of efforts to eliminate war by conquest, and the elimination of all ruling groups except the one that is victorious, does not lend much support to the theory that the *pax Bolshevika* would endure for a long time, or that it would be proof against the conflict of interests among the various elements that must necessarily be included under the term proletariat.

II

There is no particular reason why a Christian bishop should be versed in the atheistic and materialistic writings of Marxian socialism. Therefore, he is not to be seriously blamed for thinking that the Russian government has an ideal before it, even though the leaders of that government would be the first to repudiate such an insinuation. But to go further than this and say that Russia is the *only* country that has an ideal is going pretty far. He ought at least to understand what is going on in his own country. The fact is that this is one country that has a very definite and practicable, and at the same time a very beautiful ideal before it — an ideal that is vastly finer, more just, more righteous and withal more easily attainable than anything of which any socialist ever dreamed. In the pursuit of this ideal we are actually in this country achieving an economic revolution which, in the most literal possible sense, is the exact realization of the rule, "He that would be great among you, let him be your servant." Not only that, but we are actually working out in this country at the present time the only economic revolution in the world, — at least the only one that amounts to a hill of beans. Moreover, this revolution is being brought about without any help whatsoever from the professional reformers, or the preachers of purely emotional righteousness. It is being brought about by the schoolma'ams and the business men primarily, though everybody who does really good and honest work in any field of useful endeavor and who thinks clearly and votes sanely has his part in it. This is the way most great revolutions come. Those that bring great and permanent benefits to mankind usually come quietly, without noise or tumult. Many people are unconscious that a change is taking place until they suddenly realize that they are living in a new world. Writers who try to describe the change frequently resort to the device of putting some one into a Rip Van Winkle sleep during the period of change. When he awakes, his perplexity impresses the reader with the magnitude of the change. Thus the seven sleepers of Ephesus awoke to find Christianity where paganism had been.

Just what is going on in this country at the present time? Wealth is not only increasing at a rapid rate, but the wages of those we formerly pitied are rising, laborers are becoming capitalists, and prosperity is being more and more widely diffused. We are approaching equality of prosperity more rapidly than most people realize. What is equally important, we are working out this diffusion of prosperity for all classes without surrendering the principle of liberty which is embodied in modern democratic institutions.

This is a revolution which no professional reformer has ever believed possible, and which not many of them believe to be possible even now, while it is going on under their very eyes. Even Bertrand Russell, socialist intellectual, in his "Proposed Roads to Freedom", considers several other possible lines of what might be called progress, but does not even mention the possibility of the only one that is actually succeeding. There have been reformers who thought that we could have freedom of contract or voluntary agreement among free citizens as the way of getting things done, but who have maintained that if we hold to this ideal, we must give up any ideal of equality; that the penalty for this kind of freedom is the poverty of the masses and the enrichment of the few. There have been others who thought it quite possible to achieve something like equality of prosperity for all classes; but the penalty for this would be the surrender of freedom of contract or voluntary agreement among free citizens as the method of coördinating the efforts of large numbers of people. First-rate economists and far-seeing business and professional men who do not know that they are reformers, but who, after all, are the real reformers, have generally believed in the possibility of equality under freedom. No professional reformer has ever even discussed the possibility of having both these good things in combination: namely, freedom of contract with wide diffusion of prosperity among all classes. And yet we are achieving this result definitely and rather rapidly in this country at the present time.

Just what is meant by economic equality? There are several different ideas. The most general and at the same time the most practical idea is equality of prosperity among occupations. Within a given occupation there may be great differences of prosperity, owing to differences in industry, personal skill, intelligence or training. If one bricklayer can lay twice as many bricks in a day as another, it would not be equality if they received the same wages per day. One would be getting twice as much per unit of work done as the other. Yet if they are paid in proportion to their skill or industry, or if they receive equal pay for equal work, there will be personal inequality within the occupation of the bricklayer because one person would receive more than another. If one actor is a much better actor than another, it would be in harmony with a rational idea of equality that the one should be rewarded more highly than the other. The equality would consist in equal pay for work of equal quality, not in equal personal incomes. To be sure, the reward need not necessarily take the form of money. Nevertheless, it would not be a reward unless it was something that the actor wanted. If he would be satisfied with applause he might receive his reward in that form. But, it must be noted, if one receives more applause than another, there would still be inequality of reward as between a popular and an unpopular actor. If he is not entirely satisfied with applause but wants money, the actor would not be adequately rewarded unless he received money; and if different actors receive rewards in proportion to the satisfaction they render, there will be personal inequality among actors. Similarly, there would continue to be, under the same conditions, personal inequalities among lawyers, doctors, business men, writers of books, painters of pictures, and so on, even though they all received equal pay for equal services. So long as the inequalities are of this personal sort and are found within a given occupation, most of us would be satisfied; that is, if those who ply one occupation were about as prosperous on the average as those who ply any other occupation, there might be said to be equality among occupations.

As to occupational equality, there are also several things that ought to be said. If, in one occupation a man can begin earning his wages at the age of eighteen or twenty, and in another it takes so much training and experience that he really does not begin to earn much until he is thirty or thirty-five, there should be considerable difference in the annual income to compensate for the difference in the time and cost of acquiring training and experience. Again, if the risk of failure in one occupation is very small and in another very great, there should also be some compensation for this risk, otherwise the hazardous occupation would be less prosperous than the safe one.

An imaginary test might be applied to determine whether there is equality of prosperity between two occupations. Let us imagine a young man with considerable versatility, who is equally competent to turn his hand to one occupation or to the other, but is possessed of no extraordinary or peculiar ability for either. He has the time and the opportunity to secure all the training that the schools afford, and he is also perfectly informed as to all the conditions surrounding each occupation, — the money income that could be expected and the risk of failure; the honor and esteem and the other desirable things that go with each occupation. Let us imagine him trying to decide between the two, as to which offers, all things considered, the greater sum of attractions. In one occupation his chance of failure is very small; in the other it is much larger. In one the surroundings are less agreeable than in the other. One carries with it a little more honor or social esteem than the other. One requires a long period of training; the other a short period. If, after considering all the ins and outs of both occupations, he still has difficulty in deciding which to attempt, we might then say that the two occupations were equally prosperous, or that the sum total of rewards of all kinds, material and immaterial, in the two were about equal.

And yet, if we make a comparison of the incomes of those actually engaged in each occupation, we might find considerable difference. We would probably overlook, in our case-counting method, those who tried one occupation and failed, and had to turn to something else. They would not be enumerated by the ordinary statistician. We would only count those who remained in the occupation, and the only ones that remained would be those who succeeded. If we only count the successes and forget the failures it might appear as though the incomes in one occupation were much higher than in the other; and yet, according to the test we have just proposed, the superhumanly versatile and omniscient young man might have considerable difficulty in deciding between the two. To be concrete, there are a few movie actors who receive immense incomes. If one were to study their cases alone and forget the thousands of failures, one might easily jump to the conclusion that acting for the movies is one of the most prosperous of all occupations. One would soon be disillusioned if one attempted to break into the ranks of movie actors and did not possess the scarce qualities that are necessary for success.

Of course there is no such versatile person as the one we have assumed. Even if there were, he would not find any occupation so very hazardous. That is to say, if he really were as well adapted to the occupation of the movie actor as to that of the unskilled laborer, movie acting would not be, for him, so very hazardous. The same may be said regarding any other occupation in which the percentage of failures among those who attempt it is very large. For the average man, such an occupation would be hazardous. In fact his chance of failure might be so great as to amount to a certainty. But for the extraordinary man, whose qualities fit him preëminently for that particular occupation, the chance of failure may be so small as to be negligible. We are here assuming, however, that in one case the man is *really* of mediocre ability, and in the other, that he is *really* an extraordinary man who is peculiarly adapted to the occupation in question. As a matter of fact, no one really knows in advance whether he is of average fitness, or of extraordinary fitness for a given occupation. When he is in the act of choosing an occupation, and does not yet know what peculiar qualities he may possess, one occupation may really look more hazardous than another. Such a young man might well hesitate between an occupation in which there were many actual failures and a few conspicuous successes, with very large rewards, and another occupation in which there were relatively few actual failures, and no conspicuous successes with large rewards. The hazard involved in choosing the former occupation is based upon his ignorance of his own latent powers. If we assume him to have extraordinary fitness for that occupation, then, of course, the risk of failure is not so very great; but a young and untried man could not safely assume that he had extraordinary ability.

The kind of equality toward which we are progressing pretty rapidly in this country is equality among occupations, not equality of personal incomes within a given occupation. The wages of manual labor are high and are going higher. As between the manual trades and the "white collar" jobs of the mediocre sort there is practical equality now. In fact, some of the "white collar" workers have fallen to a lower level of prosperity than some of the manual workers; but the process of readjustment is still going on. It will not be long until, all things considered, the manual trades will be about as prosperous as the learned professions. As between the manual trades and the "white collar" jobs on one side, and independent business careers on the other, there is much less inequality than sometimes appears on the surface.

Probably the most hazardous of all occupations, or the occupation in which the risk of failure is highest, is that of the independent business man, whether his business be agriculture, merchandising, manufacturing or transportation. As between the farmer, let us say, and the farm hand, the former takes the greater chances. He does not know, when he puts seed in the ground, whether it will germinate or not. If it germinates, there are a thousand dangers that beset his crop before it is matured. Even then the market fluctuations keep him guessing. He does n't know what he is going to get for his crop until he has sold it and pocketed the money. The farm hand is in a much safer position. If our versatile and well-informed young man, considering the two occupations of farm hand and farmer, has great difficulty in deciding which offers the greater sum of attractions, we could say that the two occupations are about equally prosperous; and yet the few successful farmers who guessed right and who were lucky in matters of weather, insect pests, markets, etc., might show considerably larger incomes than farm hands. We would need to balance their incomes, however, against the large number of losses that came to the farmers who guessed wrong or who were unlucky regarding those unpredictable events on which success in farming depends.

Similarly, in comparing an independent business career in any field with that of a salaried or wage position, we may find, upon careful analysis, that there is a greater approximation to equality than we had previously surmised, especially if, in our previous surmises, we had never taken into account the risk of failure in business. If we count only the conspicuous successes in business, there would seem to be great inequality as between the independent business man and his employees, whether of the salaried or of the wage-earning classes. Yet, when balanced by the numerous losses, the inequalities will prove to be much smaller than was surmised. Even in these cases it might sometimes puzzle our versatile and well-informed young man who was trying to decide whether to go into business for himself or to accept a salaried position under some one else.

There are real inequalities as between occupations, but these inequalities are in the main due to the congestion of certain occupations or the oversupply of men in them and the scarcity of men in other occupations. For forty years preceding the Great War we were importing manual laborers, literally by the millions. We were not importing any very large number of employers or capitalists. This alone tended to increase the competition for jobs in the manual trades and to increase the opportunities for employers to get laborers at low wages.

While all these factors are to be taken into account in trying to determine whether there is equality of prosperity among the different occupations, and while there will always be difference of opinion as to whether such equality actually exists or not, there can be no doubt that such equality is desirable if it can be attained. It has always been the dream of real Americans that we should achieve this type of equality. We have hoped and expected that in this country of the fair chance and the square deal, every worker, whatever his occupation, should be prosperous, provided he were capable of doing good work in that occupation. We have not expected that in the same occupation the capable and the incapable, the industrious and the lazy, the dependable and the undependable should enjoy the same degree of prosperity. We have always felt real concern if farmers were poor while townsmen were rich, or *vice versa;* if laborers were poor while employers were rich; if teachers as a class were underpaid while some other class, no more meritorious, was overpaid. Recent experience may seem to fall far short of a realization of this ideal, but it has been a genuine ideal ever since the beginning of our national life.

Whatever may be said of the present or the recent past, there can be no doubt that this high idealism illumined the practical common sense of the American people from the beginning. This was to be a land of freedom, not only from monarchical rule but also from aristocratic traditions. It was to be the land of the fair chance for everybody, the land where every man could rise as high in government, in business and in social life as his character and achievements would justify. His success was to be limited only by his own ability and industry. The road from log cabin to White House was to be as open as that from palatial home to White House. The child of the laborer was to have as many and as good opportunities for his education as the child of the merchant prince. Realization may have fallen short of this noble ideal, but the ideal was cherished, and sincere efforts were made to realize it. Moreover, these efforts have met with some degree of success.

No one who really understood the American people ever doubted that this was a genuine ideal or that it amounted to a passion with many of our ancestors. It may have been crudely expressed, flamboyant orators may have torn it to tatters on Fourth of July platforms, Americans may have been somewhat stridently boastful in parading it in the presence of foreigners and in expressing some contempt for their tolerance of kings, queens, and aristocracies. All this may have shocked the taste of the *intelligentsia*, but the passion for democratic equality before the law, for the open road to virtue, industry, and talent, for the fair chance and the square deal, was as genuine as it was vocal.

In the main, the policies of the government were gradually brought into harmony with this noble ideal. The development of our public land policy is a case in point. It began as a means of replenishing an empty treasury, but it rapidly grew into a plan for giving free homesteads to all citizens who cared to settle on public land and build themselves farms and homes. Land was early made a merchantable commodity, entailed estates were made impossible in the lands that once belonged to the Federal Government, and most of the original thirteen States followed the national policy. Our system of free popular education is another case. Though it was, for constitutional reasons, left mainly to the States, yet the States generally took measures to put a school within the reach, both geometrically and financially, of every family. In these measures they were encouraged and in some cases aided by the Federal Government.

Moreover, this ideal was made flesh in the persons of our most popular leaders. The most revered of these leaders were those who put this ideal most vividly into words or most dramatically into action. Only three outstanding names need be mentioned: Jefferson, Clay, and Lincoln. Both Jefferson and

Clay were led as by a beatific vision to work for a great democracy where every man was the political equal of every other; where no one had any advantage in the race for prosperity except his own inherent ability or character; where every man could choose his own occupation and seek the one in which, all things considered, he could achieve the greatest prosperity. It was the hope and belief that this would lead to practical equality of prosperity among all occupations. It was inconceivable that free men should, in any considerable number, deliberately choose those occupations that led to poverty, while other occupations that led to prosperity were open to them. By the time of Lincoln this ideal seemed in process of being realized, except in the case of the negro slaves. We had already become a great and glorious nation without the aid, or the encumbrance, of a monarch or a ruling caste. To ardent democrats this seemed like a spiritual triumph. The thought of it produced a feeling of spiritual exaltation akin to, if not better than, religious ecstasy. The writer herewith bears testimony to the fact that he and the other young fellows of the generation immediately following the Civil War actually experienced this sort of spiritual exaltation whenever they contemplated the achievements of this great democracy.

It is a matter for eternal regret that few present-day writers have ever entered fully into the thoughts and feelings of the common people of this period.

Of necessity they belong to the sophisticated class, and sophistication too often robs us of our appreciation of the virile qualities of our American democracy. There have been a few exceptions, notable among whom is Winston Churchill, whose remarkable book, "The Crisis", is a revelation of the inner heart of this early American democracy. It is difficult to select any passage which, more than any other, voices this revelation. Speaking of the interest of a typical prairie farmer in the Lincoln-Douglass debate, he says: [1]

"This son of toil who had driven his family thirty miles across the prairie, blanketed his tired horses and slept on the ground the night before, who was willing to stand all through the afternoon and listen with pathetic eagerness to this debate, must be moved by a patriotism divine. In the breast of that farmer, in the breast of his tired wife who held her child by the hand, had been instilled from birth that sublime fervor which is part of their life who inherit the Declaration of Independence. Instinctively these men who had fought and won the West had scented the danger. With the spirit of their ancestors who had left their farms to die on the bridge at Concord, or follow Ethan Allen into Ticonderoga, these had come to Freeport. What were three days of bodily discomfort! What even the loss of part of a cherished crop, if the nation's existence were at stake and their votes might save it!"

[1] Page 154. The Macmillan Company. New York, 1907.

Another writer of profound insight, in the days of his youthful enthusiasm, wrote as follows[1] of the people who subdued the continent and made it the nursing mother of a virile democracy:

"It was an awkward, cumbersome business to subdue a continent in such wise, — hard to plan, and very likely impossible to execute. Under such circumstances Nature was much bigger and stronger than man. She would suffer no sudden highways to be thrown across her spaces; she abated not an inch of her mountains, compromised not a foot of her forests. Still, she did not daunt the designs of the new nation born on the sea-edge of her wilds. Here is the secret, — a secret so open, it would seem, as to baffle the penetration of none, — which many witnesses of the material growth and territorial expansion of the United States have strangely failed to divine. The history of the country and the ambitions of its people have been deemed both sordid and mean, inspired by nothing better than a desire for the gross comforts of material abundance; and it has been pronounced grotesque that mere bigness and wealth should be put forward as the most prominent grounds for the boast of greatness. The obvious fact is that for the creation of the nation the conquest of her proper territory from Nature was first necessary; and this task, which is hardly yet completed, has been idealized in the popular mind.

[1] *See* Woodrow Wilson's "Division and Reunion", page 3. Longmans, Green and Co., New York, 1921.

A bold race has derived inspiration from the size, the difficulty, the danger of the task.

"Expansion has meant nationalization; nationalization has meant strength and elevation of view.

> Be strong-backed, brown-handed, upright as your pines;
> By the scale of a hemisphere shape your designs,

is the spirited command of enthusiasm for the great physical undertaking upon which political success was conditioned."

During all this period faith in the people meant the belief that every American was capable of taking care of himself and did not need paternalistic help. The results of this policy seem to justify the belief. There came a time later when this faith in the individual was severely shaken. Conditions arose under which it seemed that thousands or even millions of individuals were unable to shift for themselves successfully. Men and women of little faith began to despair of liberty and to proclaim that our boasted liberty too frequently meant the liberty to starve. A little more insight would have convinced them that liberty is always a dangerous thing. It has its penalties, but it is worth what it costs. Sophists began to juggle with words to show that liberty did not mean what it obviously did mean,— freedom from authority and control by other human beings, — but that it meant freedom from the coercion of circumstances. No one ever dreamed that freedom consisted in escaping from the control of circumstances. It has always meant, and still means, freedom from control by human authority. Others have argued that it means freedom from poverty, and, being ignorant of economic principles, have assumed that there is some antithesis between freedom from authority and freedom from poverty; and that we must choose between these two forms of so-called freedom because we cannot possibly have both. The older American ideal was that we could have both. As a matter of fact, we were actually achieving both.

Still other writers, during the period of mass poverty, began to assert that the older individualistic ideal must give way to a newer social ideal, forgetting that the so-called social ideal was old and outworn before the individualistic ideal ever became dominant. They were accustomed to point to the masses of poverty among the recently arrived immigrants, who had not yet become adjusted, as proof that our boasted liberty from authority was a failure, and to say that the exercise of government authority was a necessity in order to enable the masses of people who could not take care of themselves to achieve some degree of prosperity. They could not see that it was the oversupply of the labor market by the importation of millions of cheap laborers that was the chief factor in the difficulty; that if this disturbing factor could be removed, the ability of the average citizen to take care of himself would again be demonstrated; that through our system of popular education, insuring to every young person as much education as he is capable of taking on, and leaving to each one a free choice of occupations, the general avoidance of the underpaid occupations and seeking of the well-paid occupations would so distribute our population occupationally as to create something approximating to equality of prosperity among them all. They could not see that the failure to do this was due to the fact that millions of workers came to us without having had this opportunity for the free choice of occupations.

They could, however, support their claims by pointing to old countries with aristocratic traditions, and show that even there, where there was no immigration, there was still occupational congestion in the manual trades. This failure to note the difference between equality of opportunity and inequality of opportunity, reveals complete inability on their part to understand what had actually been going on in this country and what American ideals really were. We have not been handicapped by aristocratic traditions and hereditary class distinctions as they have.

During the last half-dozen years, since we have removed the disturbing factor, or greatly reduced it — that is, the importation of vast numbers of unskilled laborers — we are gradually relieving the occupational congestion under which we suffered for at least two generations. Since we have relieved ourselves of this burden, we are once more beginning to demonstrate that under freedom, that is — freedom from authority — and with free opportunity, men will regularly and of their own volition avoid the underpaid and seek the well-paid occupations. In so far as they avoid the underpaid occupations, they tend to make labor scarce in those occupations, and this tends to raise wages. It tends also to diffuse prosperity among all classes. Since the restriction of immigration, we have already progressed far enough to enable a few to look forward to a revival of the old, healthy and virile American individualism. A few are beginning to be convinced that we can have freedom from authority combined with freedom from poverty and that we are not compelled to choose between the two.

Those earlier ideals have been all but obscured during the last two generations. Even most of the recent biographies of Lincoln have been written by people whose brain paths were formed during this period of obscuration. Consequently, these biographies are filled with the mawkish social sentiments that came into existence in this country after Lincoln's day, while we were struggling with the problem of relieving the distress of multitudes of manual workers whose distress was the clear and indubitable product of an overcrowded labor market.

To one who knows nothing of the idealism of

that earlier day, when men believed in both equality and liberty and saw in this country the realization, for the first time in history, of that noble ideal, it is incomprehensible that people should have cared intensely for the preservation of the nation that was then in process of realizing that ideal. No one understands Lincoln's attitude toward secession who does not know something of this feeling. To one who knows nothing of it, Horace Greeley's advice, "Let the erring sisters depart in peace", seems eminently sensible. If the people of the North had not known this feeling and the idealism that begat it, North and South might have separated as peacefully as Norway and Sweden did a few decades later. But, in this country, that simply could not be. To have lost the splendid vision of a great and glorious nation of free men would have been to experience spiritual bereavement; to have seen it broken up would have been to experience spiritual amputation. It was more than our people could stand; though there were, of course, then as now, cynics who mocked at such feelings.

Such was the idealism of the American people during the first century of our national life. Then came the great slump.

In a sense our very idealism was our undoing. Our idealism produced its own poison that almost destroyed it. This had become the land of opportunity, the land of the fair chance and the square deal, the land to which the oppressed of other nations could come and free themselves of all handicaps, and succeed according to their merits. The revolutions of the late forties on the continent and the potato famine in Ireland had already induced large numbers to come and to enter into this new experience. Shortly after the Civil War others began to come, and in increasing numbers. At first they sought the western lands.

A combination of factors worked together at this period to produce the greatest agricultural depression of modern times. To begin with, the transcontinental railroads were built in advance of agricultural settlement, making it easy for settlers to reach the western lands. Previously, going west and settling on public lands had been a formidable enterprise, involving some weeks of traveling in a prairie schooner and months of hardship in a cabin, shut off by lack of transportation from the comforts of eastern life. Now transportation to the land was swift and easy, and the railroads could bring many of the comforts of civilization to the western settlers. In the second place, the roller process of manufacturing flour made it possible to make excellent flour of the spring wheat which was adapted to the prairies of the great Northwest. Before this, agricultural experts were pessimistic as to the possibility of extending the growing of spring wheat. Now it was possible to market it in indefinite quantities at a price, though the price fell to unprofitable levels. Without this, it probably could not have been sold at any price. In the third place, the twine binder and the steam thresher greatly reduced the cost of harvesting and threshing the wheat. In the fourth place, and most important of all, the Homestead Law, passed during the Civil War, gave a quarter section (one hundred and sixty acres) of land, without money and without price, to the actual settler who would live on the land and farm it. This applied to immigrants who declared their intention of becoming citizens, and millions of them began to come. Improved implements for the planting and cultivation of corn and the extension of the cattle business in advance of agriculture over the great plains of the West came at the same time.

The net result of all these changes was such an expansion of the agricultural area as the modern world had never seen. During the decade from 1870 to 1880, over 297,000 square miles were added to the cultivated area of the United States. This was an area equal in extent to Great Britain and France combined. The population of the grain States of the Northwest increased more than forty-two per cent. During this same decade the immigration to the United States amounted to nearly three million persons. During the decade from 1880 to 1890 the number of immigrants reached the astonishing number of five and a quarter million. The increase in the leading crops of the Northwest is shown by the following table from the United States census.

	Corn, bushels	Wheat, bushels	Oats, bushels
1839	377,531,875	84,823,272	123,071,341
1849	592,071,104	100,485,944	146,584,179
1859	838,792,742	173,104,924	172,643,185
1869	760,944,549	287,745,626	282,107,157
1879	1,754,591,676	459,483,137	407,858,999
1889	2,122,327,547	468,373,968	809,250,666
1899	2,666,440,279	658,534,252	943,389,375

The pouring of this flood of agricultural products on to the markets of the world produced a veritable agricultural cataclysm. Farmers, not only in the eastern part of the United States but in European countries as well, felt the depression. The abandoned farms of the East began to attract attention. Farmers everywhere were discontented and restless. Whereas through most of the history of the past, the agricultural population of every country had been looked upon as stable and little given to radicalism, now our own agricultural States became the seedbed of radicalism. The grange movement, though started as a constructive movement for improving agricultural products and the living conditions of farmers, rapidly became a political movement for the relief of the farmers through political measures. After nearly wrecking itself through unwise political action, the grange returned to sanity and became an organization for constructive action. Its period of radicalism, however, was followed by a series of other movements of the same kind. The greenback movement of the seventies and early eighties resisted the deflation made necessary by the resumption of the gold standard. After the futility of this resistance was demonstrated, the free silver movement and the populist movement succeeded in swift succession.

As invariably happens, the blame for the condition of the farmers was improperly placed. It was obviously due to the fact that there were too many farmers, and there was obviously no cure for the situation until the number of consumers of agricultural products increased sufficiently to balance the number of producers. But the blame was laid on the railroads, the banks, the "money power", and every other factor in our economic life which the farmers did not quite understand. Wherever there is anything that is not clearly understood, it is invariably an object of suspicion.

With the practical exhaustion of the public lands, the expansion of the farm area slowed down. And from the late nineties to the outbreak of the Great War, a gradual improvement in agricultural conditions was noticeable. With this improvement, radicalism among the farmers became quiescent and remained so until another agricultural depression in the wheat belt, due to the rapid expansion of wheat growing in the Canadian Northwest, produced the Nonpartisan League. The reason for the agricultural revival from the late nineties to the outbreak of the Great War was that the only effective cure for the situation was in operation. The consumption of agricultural products was increasing rapidly enough gradually to overtake production.

The following chart from the Yearbook of the United States Department of Agriculture for 1923, page 72, shows how the crop area increased or decreased relatively to population from 1880 to 1920.

Trend in Per Capita Acreage of Crops, Pasture, and Forest, and Amount of Livestock, United States, 1880–1920

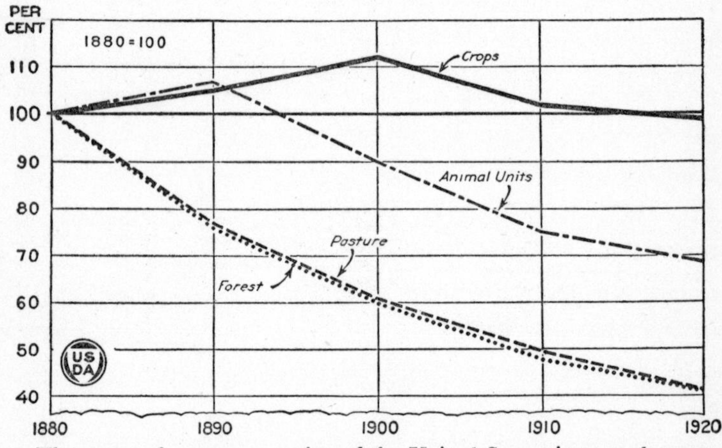

The acres of crops per capita of the United States increased 12 per cent. between 1880 and 1900, and then decreased to an amount in 1920 1 per cent. below that in 1880. The per capita acreages of both pasture and forest land, on the other hand, have declined since 1880, and are now only 40 per cent. as great as forty years ago. The per capita amount of livestock increased till 1890, and has since decreased at almost as rapid a rate as pasture.

According to this, the crop acreage increased more rapidly than the population from 1880 to 1900, since which time it has been declining. This explains very clearly why farm prices were depressed prior to 1900 and why they gradually improved from 1900 to 1914. The conditions since 1914 were so violently disturbed by the war as to make the diagram mean little for this period. The rapid expansion of wheat growing in Western Canada during recent years is of course not shown in this diagram. If it were, it would help to explain the depression in wheat prices from 1920 to 1924, though even this could not show the decline in the purchasing power of our best European customers.

The decline in pasturage and animal units began about 1890. This decline in animal units, however, has been somewhat compensated by the more rapid turnover, that is, the fattening and marketing of meat animals at a somewhat younger age.

But another problem of the same kind developed in an entirely different quarter. Immigrants continued to come, but since there was no longer sufficient land of good quality to attract them, they crowded into our cities and factory towns. This did for the labor market precisely what the earlier immigration had done for the agricultural market. Laborers were generally oversupplied and the price of labor was depressed relatively to other shares just as the price of agricultural products had been depressed from 1880 to 1900. The seedbed of radicalism was transferred from the western farms to the eastern shops, and this for obvious reasons. It is obvious that there was no real cure for the agricultural situation of the eighties and nineties except a restoration of the balance, a slowing down of agricultural expansion and the increase of urban population to consume farm products. We have actually seen this cure in operation, and most of us are able to understand it now. We can sometimes understand a thing when we are shown, even though we are not convinced by argument. To those who really understand, it is equally obvious that the only cure for the labor situation that developed as the result of the overcrowding of our towns and factories was of the same kind. There was no real cure for it except a restoration of the balance, but in this, as in the other case, all sorts of radical cures have been suggested and some have been tried. We have had a perfect orgy of social legislation, all of which is applied to the symptoms rather than to the cause of the trouble.

The former depression of the agricultural market was a positive advantage to large numbers of consumers of agricultural products. They could buy cheap food; in fact, most of it was bought below cost. When, in the early years of the present century, the price of agricultural products began to rise somewhat more rapidly than the price of other things, the former beneficiaries of the agricultural depression began to be disturbed over the high cost of living.

They did not realize that the trouble was not really the high cost of living. The trouble was that they had become accustomed to an abnormally low cost. The prices of agricultural products were only getting back to a fair normal, that is, a level that would yield a fair income to the producers of these crops. In short, so far as the occupation of farming was concerned, we were once more beginning to realize the great American ideal of prosperity for all classes. The class, namely the farming class, that had been suffering from over production, was emerging from that state and sharing in the prosperity of the country as a whole.

The more recent depression of the labor market was also to the advantage of certain other classes. If we may group the business and professional classes together and speak of them as the employing classes, they were all benefited by an abundant supply of cheap labor. It enabled the white collar people to live better than they could have lived if manual labor had been scarce. Others became inordinately prosperous by buying this cheap labor, organizing it for effective production, and selling the product at a good profit. So great became the disparity between the prosperity of the manual workers and the employing classes that many of our people forgot the real American ideal, grew pessimistic, or thought that we had no ideal in this country. But there were always a few who were able to see deeper than the surface and to realize that, in spite of this temporary obscuration, we were still doing a great deal for labor. To take half a million laborers a year for a period of years, coming to us from a state of poverty, bringing nothing but their two hands, and put them on the road to prosperity was no small achievement. Superficial observers pointed to the slums of our cities and were impressed by their permanency. They did not look closely enough to see that, though the slums continued, the personnel of the slums changed. The slums were like a reservoir, fed by one stream and drained by another. The reservoir seems to be permanent, though the water changes. The newly arrived immigrants formed the stream that fed the slums. Their promotion to positions that brought greater economic prosperity was the stream that drained the slums. This ought to have been, and was to those who understood it, ground for optimism. The same factors that enabled us to take vast numbers of laborers from abroad and give them jobs, even at wages distressingly low, but somewhat better than other countries could pay them, would obviously have enabled us to take care of a smaller number of laborers on somewhat better terms; that is, to pay them somewhat higher wages and give them somewhat better conditions. The soundness of our economic and political institutions was indicated by the fact that we kept the factors active that tend to increase the demand for labor. Even though the supply of labor came to us so rapidly as to place a great strain upon the system, nevertheless the system was functioning admirably; otherwise we could not possibly have taken care of so many surplus laborers from other and less progressive countries.

What is fundamentally the same remedy as that which brought agriculture out of the depression of the eighties and nineties into the relative prosperity of the first fourteen years of the present century is already at work, lifting our laboring classes out of the depression that followed the vast immigration preceding the Great War. The war itself practically stopped immigration from other continents, but not from Mexico, and the restriction laws since the war have prevented its rising to pre-war levels. The same factors are now at work giving better conditions to our own laborers that were formerly at work giving rather poor conditions to a vast surplus of laborers from abroad. So far as the manual workers are concerned, we are again beginning to realize the old ideal of sound Americans, — equal prosperity for all classes and occupations, and that too, under liberty. The most serious menace at the present time is that of bootlegging in men, the bringing of immigrants over the Canadian and the Mexican borders. There is already an acute need for restriction of immigration from Mexico — a country that is doing nothing to provide better conditions for its own laborers and will continue to shift that burden on to us, so long as we are willing to accept it. We are rapidly creating another race problem by the wholesale importation of Mexican peons.

To those who belittle this economic achievement as a materialistic ideal, or speak in derogatory terms of our American achievements in this direction, I can offer, as a sufficient answer, the following quotation from Ruskin: [1]

One day last November, at Oxford, as I was going in at the private door of the University galleries, to give a lecture on the Fine Arts in Florence, I was hindered for a moment by a nice little girl, whipping a top on the pavement. She was a *very* nice little girl; and rejoiced wholly in her whip, and top; but could not inflict the reviving chastisement with all the activity that was in her, because she had on a large and dilapidated pair of woman's shoes, which projected the full length of her own little foot behind it and before; and being securely fastened to her ankles in the manner of moccasins, admitted, indeed, of dextrous glissades, and other modes of progress quite sufficient for ordinary purposes; but not conveniently of all the evolutions proper to the pursuit of a whipping-top.

There were some worthy people at my lecture, and I think the lecture was one of my best. It gave some really trustworthy information about art in

[1] From John Ruskin's "Fors Clavigera", Vol. II, Letter XXXVII.

Florence six hundred years ago. But all the time I was speaking, I knew that nothing spoken about art, either by myself or other people, could be of the least use to anybody there. For their primary business, and mine, was with art in Oxford, now; not with art in Florence, then; and art in Oxford now was absolutely dependent on our power of solving the question — which I knew that my audience would not even allow to be proposed for solution — "Why have our little girls large shoes?"

We are rapidly creating a condition in this country under which little girls do not need to wear big shoes. We are leading all other countries in this direction. It is, of course, deplorable that we cannot do a number of other things at the same time. The writer wishes that we could also lead the other countries in the Fine Arts. It seems to some to be desirable that we should lead them in those arts that usually go with squalor, dirt, and display, which some particularly frank Mediævalists seem to prefer to anything modern. But even though we do fall behind in those arts that are commonly cultivated by a leisure class, and that require a leisure class for their proper cultivation, we may take a certain genuine satisfaction in the fact that we have no leisure class and are never likely to have one. We must therefore content ourselves with such arts and graces as can be cultivated by busy people.

A shrewd observer and a keen analyst has recently said:[1]

I have long felt that the chief contribution of the United States to progress has been in the wide distribution of what may be called the "good things of life."

In learning, in culture, and in the fine art of living, we have probably not reached the peaks of many earlier and even some modern nations.

As we learn more of ancient civilizations we come to realize that the Egyptians, Babylonians, Greeks, and Romans lived richly, thought deeply and cultivated the best that life offers. That is, the select few did. The mass of people existed in hopeless slavery, their lot being no better than that of common beasts of burden.

In the United States we teach the idea that the door of opportunity is open to all.

Probably we have not yet reared a man with an intellect equal in power and penetration to that of Aristotle, but we have, with free universal education, almost eliminated illiteracy. All of us know the fundamentals, even though none of us knows as much as the greatest of the Greeks.

We have few roads equal in construction to those built two thousand years ago by the Romans, but we have more roads and superior facilities of transportation. Through our postal, telegraph, and railroad

[1] From the *William Feather Magazine* for November, 1924. Published by The William Feather Company, Cleveland, Ohio.

systems, communication and travel are cheap and easy, and open to all.

The tables of the Egyptian kings were heaped with delicacies, gathered from all parts of the known world, but their subjects lived on scant rations of coarse, rough food.

Poetry was written, sculpture carved, temples were constructed, fabrics woven, and plays presented — for the rulers and their sycophants. But for the masses there was no hope. They were not considered in the scheme of things.

When we visit art museums to-day and inspect the craftsmanship exhibited in articles more than a thousand years old, we are shamed by the comparison with our modern factory-made products.

It is only on second thought, when we realize that a few centuries ago only kings enjoyed the luxuries which are to-day common necessities, that we get the proper thrill from twentieth-century achievements.

This, then, I believe to be the great contribution of America: a universal education through public schools, universal access to all literature through public libraries, universal opportunity for communication through cheap postal rates, and finally, universal enjoyment of comforts and conveniences through a factory system which supplies goods at a price so low that many millions to-day live in comparative luxury.

The development of a free and democratic form of government which has been established in this country would mean little if it had not been accompanied by an improvement in living standards. . . .

The vision of the majority of American manufacturers is to produce products which shall be universally used — to make goods so well and so cheap that they may find a place in every home.

This is a democratic vision.

Our advertising and salesmanship are tuned to the democratic idea.

Our manufacturers do not advertise "Purveyors to His Majesty", which is a snobbish and an exclusive appeal. The American slogan is "Used in every home" and "A million satisfied users."

In no other country have merchants and manufacturers caught this idea because their "markets" are circumscribed by centuries of thinking in terms of "royalty" and "upper classes." In the United States the market consists of "the population" — every human being is regarded as a potential customer.

To supply goods for this mass of purchasing power, a low level of quality might seem inevitable, and yet few manufacturers have ever succeeded in obtaining national distribution of goods of low quality, no matter how low the price. In striving for the national market millions of dollars are wasted in the production of goods that might better never have been made. It is a waste of honest labor to manufacture shoddy, flimsy goods, and a waste of money to buy them.

The modern ideal is high quality and low price.

American manufacturers are proving this is possible through quantity production and distribution — through offering good things to everybody and teaching everybody to want good things.

The contrast between the achievements of this country and those of the countries of Western Europe is, of course, not so wide as that between any of these modern countries on the one hand and ancient and mediæval countries on the other. We can truly say, however, that in this modern achievement of wide diffusion of prosperity under liberty, this country has gone farther than any other. To have realized such a wide diffusion of prosperity as Mr. Feather describes is no mean achievement. The nation that succeeds in thus making real the noble ideals of liberty and equality in combination need not hang its head in shame before any nation that has made any other contribution to civilization — however great and worthy. The writer personally takes more satisfaction and pride in living in a country that has realized this great ideal than he could take if his country had failed in this respect and done anything that any other country has ever done. Of course it would be perfectly magnificent to have achieved what we have and also—if that were possible — what other great nations have achieved.

This wide diffusion of prosperity has, as might have been anticipated, many penalties. Among other things it has put a vast aggregate of purchasing power in the hands of millions of men and women of low mentality and coarse tastes. This vast reservoir of purchasing power provides a market for the producers and sellers of the kinds of goods and services that appeal to such people. Even the advertisements that cover the pages of our cheap periodicals are designed to appeal to people of the same level. In other countries, such people would not have money enough to make them interesting to sellers and advertisers; they would be typical proletarians. Here they are the bourgeoisie, at least in their purchasing power.

Again, such people buy newspapers and magazines. The result is that many of our newspapers and magazines are edited for such people. If they did not have purchasing power, such periodicals as we had would be edited for other classes, that is, for those who, by heredity and training, were able to appreciate somewhat more refined literary products.

All this we may as well admit. Nevertheless, it is a glorious achievement to have put so much purchasing power in the possession of masses of people who, in other countries, would never have had it, — who would, in fact, have constituted the impoverished masses.

The amazing material prosperity that is coming to this country through the pursuit of the noble ideal of equality under liberty, and our failure to develop the arts of leisure, are deceiving many superficial observers into believing that our ideals are themselves materialistic. But this prosperity is coming to us precisely because our ideals are not materialistic. It is coming to us because we are pursuing the exalted ideal of equality under liberty, as it must of necessity come to any nation that pursues that ideal whole-heartedly and enthusiastically. No nation can fail to prosper, up to the limit set by its physical resources, that genuinely seeks equality under liberty. All these things are being added unto us precisely because we are seeking the Kingdom of God and his righteousness, as they are always added and must of logical necessity always be added unto any nation that seeks whole-heartedly those ideals of justice that are the very essence of the Kingdom of God.

CHAPTER THREE

The Genesis of a Labor Problem

I

THERE was once an old cattleman out in Colorado who had gone there in an early day and grown up with the business. He had worked hard, risked his life on more than one occasion, and endured hardships that would have discouraged, and in many cases did actually discourage, men of less persistence. He had lived with his business until he had become almost a part of it. As he became prosperous and his cattle increased, he hired a number of cowboys, thus becoming a fair-sized capitalist and an employer of labor. He knew his cowboys personally, called them by their first names, and never pretended to belong to a different social class, though he never left them in any doubt as to who was boss about the ranch. They sometimes called him by his first name, though among themselves, when he was not present, he was simply "the old man."

It would be useless to contend that there was no wage controversy between this capitalist employer and his laborers. There was. The cowboys were emphatic and sometimes picturesque in their declarations to the effect that they were not paid enough.

The old man was equally emphatic and even more picturesque in his statements to the effect that they were paid more than they were worth. He sometimes became personal and pointed in his remarks, telling them with all his objurgatory power that they were not worth their salt. And yet there was, strictly speaking, no labor problem; at least, there was none in the sense in which that expression is now generally used. To begin with, there was no social gap separating the employing class from the laboring class. In fact, there were no classes. Social classes are a frame of mind. No one spoke or thought in terms of class consciousness because there was no class consciousness, and since there was no class consciousness there were no classes.

The cowboys recognized the leadership of the old man; they knew that he knew more about cattle and the cattle business than they did. They would have liked to be as rich as he, but, on the other hand, they did not resent his riches. In fact, they were rather proud to be working for a man who was so successful and had become so rich in the cattle business. Every one of them was willing to defend him and his reputation against all comers in spite of the fact that when they were talking to him they were not always polite.

There was no lack of sociability between "the old man" and his cowboys. Whenever people are brought into physical contact and are in possession of a common interest, there is always social intercourse. These men all had a common interest, namely, cattle. The cattle business furnished a great variety of themes for the holding of high converse. This common interest bridged the gap between them as effectively as a common interest in religion, golf, rheumatism, or Bernard Shaw does among other people. "The old man" enjoyed their society and they enjoyed his because they were all vitally interested in the same things.

In the course of time, "the old man" waxed old in years as well as in experience. There had grown up around him a family of sons and daughters who craved the culture of the East which the family wealth could well afford. They persuaded him to move to Kansas City, where they speedily acquired interests in other things beside cattle. "The old man", however, never lost his early interest nor acquired any other. He oscillated back and forth between his city home and his ranch. He remained on familiar terms with his cowboys and enjoyed their society rather more than that of any of the citizens of that "eastern" center of culture. The wage situation remained about the same, and no labor problem developed.

After many years "the old man" was gathered to his fathers and the ranch passed into the possession of the second generation. If there was any difference in the wage situation, it was that wages were better than they had been under "the old man." Nevertheless a labor problem gradually developed. A gap began to appear between the laboring people, that is, the cowboys, and the absentee owners. It was not merely the fact of physical absence that counted, though physical absence was a factor. In addition to that there developed the lack of a common interest. There was nothing to talk about that interested both employers and employees; there was no common basis of mutual understanding and sympathy. The owners were less and less interested in cattle as such, but more and more interested in the things which the income from the ranch would purchase. The interest shifted from production to consumption. The ranch became to them, more and more, merely a source of income. It was no longer a treasure in itself. The treasures were found in various articles of consumption which they were now able to afford, and where the treasure was, there the hearts were also.

Since there was no basis for mutual understanding, appreciation, and sympathy, the wage question began to breed a new kind of opposition. It was combined with a feeling of class distinction. Employers and employees lived in different worlds because their interests were centered in different things. Where this feeling of class distinction exists it is always possible to find an issue. There are dozens of sources of irritation, any one of which may start a quarrel. The question of wages makes a very convenient issue.

In this parable (for it is a parable) we find the real explanation of the existence of a labor problem which must always be distinguished from the wage question. There is never a labor problem except where there is a feeling of class distinction. The feeling of class distinction grows up automatically whereever people with widely different interests are brought into contact. If one group of people who are peculiarly proud of the color of their skin are brought into contact with people whose skin is of another color, a feeling of class distinction will exist. If people who are vitally interested in one type of religion are brought into contact with people of another religion or of no religion at all, a feeling of class distinction will develop. If people who are inordinately proud of their culture are brought into contact with the uncultured, the same thing happens. When people whose chief interest in life is in the scale of their consumption or the lavishness with which they can entertain are brought into contact with people who have to live on another scale or who have to entertain less lavishly, we get the same result. The mere fact that one person is an employer and another an employee does not of itself produce the feeling of class distinction. A common interest in a common work unites and does not divide people. So long as the employer was primarily interested in the work of raising cattle, as was this old cattleman, his contact with his cowboys did not produce a feeling of class distinction. When a generation arose that "knew not Joseph", that lacked his constructive interest in a big job, but cared more for consumption than production, their contact with the cowboys produced a feeling of class distinction as it always does, everywhere, under similar conditions.

II

If we have class consciousness in the United States we must find the explanation here. It would seem that with our democratic traditions and our universal respect for labor, with our common-school system under which employer and employee could have gone to school together and called one another by their first names — as they probably did — such a thing as class distinction should not have arisen. It would seem that the relationship between employer and employee ought to have been, and ought still to be, like that which existed between the old man and his cowboys in the parable which we have just told. What has interfered to thrust a wedge of class consciousness between employers and laborers?

When one reads the account of some of the early factory towns of New England, such as Lowell, one finds very little in the way of class consciousness and much that resembles the relationship already referred to between "the old man" and his cowboys. Employers and employees were working together on the common task of building an industry. They had gone to the same schools, attended the same churches and had many common interests.

We can scarcely realize at this time, after fifty or more years of immigrant labor with many strikes and acute labor disputes, and the development of a distinct class consciousness, the social conditions that once prevailed in some of the New England factories, even though wages were much lower than now. An excellent account is given in "A New England Girlhood", by Lucy Larcom,[1] regarding her own life as a factory girl in Lowell. She says:

> The girls who toiled together at Lowell were clearing away a few weeds from the overgrown track of independent labor for other women. They practically said, by numbering themselves among factory girls, that in our country no real odium could be attached to any honest toil that any self-respecting woman might undertake.
>
> I regard it as one of the privileges of my youth that I was permitted to grow up among those active, interesting girls, whose lives were not mere echoes of other lives, but had principle and purpose distinctly their own. . . .
>
> I do not believe that any Lowell mill-girl was ever absurd enough to wish to be known as a "fac-

[1] Houghton, Mifflin & Company. Boston, 1889.

tory-lady", although most of them knew that "factory-girl" did not represent a high type of womanhood in the Old World. But they themselves belonged to the New World, not to the Old; and they were making their own traditions, to hand down to the Republican descendants, — one of which was and is that honest work has no need to assert itself or to humble itself in a nation like ours, but simply to take its place as one of the foundation-stones of the Republic.

The young women who worked at Lowell had the advantage of living in a community where character alone commanded respect. They never, at their work or away from it, heard themselves contemptuously spoken of on account of their occupation, except by the ignorant or weak-minded, whose comments they were of course too sensible to heed....

Work, study, and worship were interblended in our life. The church was really the home-centre to many, perhaps to most of us; and it was one of the mill regulations that everybody should go to church somewhere. There must have been an earnest group of ministers at Lowell, since nearly all the girls attended public worship from choice.

Our minister joined us in our social gatherings, often inviting us to his own house, visiting us at our work, accompanying us on our picnics down the river-bank . . . suggesting books for our reading, and assisting us in our studies.

The two magazines published by the mill-girls,

the "Lowell Offering" and the "Operatives' Magazine", originated with literary meetings in the vestry of two religious societies, the first in the Universalist Church, the second in the First Congregational, to which my sister and I belonged. . . .

In recalling those years of my girlhood at Lowell, I often think that I knew then what real society is better perhaps than ever since. For in that large gathering together of young womanhood there were many choice natures — some of the choicest in all our excellent New England, and there were no false social standards to hold them apart. . . .

As I recall the throngs of unknown girlish forms that used to pass and repass me on the familiar road to the millgates, and also the few that I knew so well, those with whom I worked, thought, read, wrote, studied, and worshipped, my thoughts send a heartfelt greeting to them all, wherever in God's beautiful, busy universe they may now be scattered. . . .

We were allowed to have books in the clothroom. The absence of machinery permitted that privilege. Our superintendent, who was a man of culture and a Christian gentleman of the Puritan-school, dignified and reserved, used often to stop at my desk in his daily round to see what I was reading. . . . It was a satisfaction to have a superintendent like him, whose granite principles, emphasized by his stately figure and bearing, made him a tower of strength in the church and in the community. He kept a silent, kindly, rigid watch over the corporation-life of which he was the head; and only those of us who were incidentally admitted to his confidence knew how carefully we were guarded. . . .

We had occasional glimpses into his own well-ordered home-life, at social gatherings. His little daughter was in my infant Sabbath-school class. . . . She sometimes visited me at my work, and we had our frolics among the heaps of cloth, as if we were both children. . . .

Occasionally a young girl was attracted to the Lowell mills through her own idealization of the life there, as it had been reported to her. Margaret Foley, who afterwards became distinguished as a sculptor, was one of these. She did not remain many months at her occupation, — which I think was weaving, — soon changing it for that of teaching and studying art. Those who came as she did were usually disappointed. Instead of an Arcadia, they found a place of matter-of-fact toil, filled with a company of industrious, wide-awake girls, who were faithfully improving their opportunities, while looking through them into avenues toward profit and usefulness, more desirable yet. It has always been the way of the steady-minded New Englander to accept the present situation, — but to accept it without boundaries, taking in also the larger prospects — all the heavens above and the earth beneath — towards which it opens.

A later writer, George F. Kenngott, at one time a minister of religion in Lowell, belonging to a generation that had known much of class conscious labor troubles, looking back on the past, writes: [1]

"There are still those in Lowell who remember the 'former days' and pine for their return — the happy days when life was homogeneous, and all were one in their loyalty to the new mill town on the Merrimack, when the Yankee girls worked leisurely thirteen hours a day in the mills and wrote poetry at night, when everybody went to church on Sunday, and worshipped God in a common tongue. It is a far cry, indeed, from the city of more than 106,000, made up of fifty or more nationalities, with fifty per cent. foreign born and eighty per cent. foreign parentage, to the days of 'auld lang syne' when all knew each other, thought the same thoughts, spoke the same language, and worshipped in the same way.

"The paternal relation of employer and employed is gone. The mill agent does not fraternize with the mill operative to-day; ofttimes he cannot if he would, for differences of race, language and habits, if not of religion, separate them. The real proprietors of the mills, the stockholders, live elsewhere, and have little thought of Lowell save to draw dividends. They have builded their tower of Babel on the banks of the Merrimack; and the pride of life, the thirst for gold, the demand for cheap labor, have brought hither a confusion of tongues that no Pentecost of love has yet transformed into a harmony of single devotion and united effort.

[1] "The Record of a City", The Macmillan Company. New York, 1912.

"The textile corporations have sold their tenements and boarding-houses. Rents have been doubled and trebled; the native Americans have moved into the suburbs or gone to other cities; the foreigners from the Far East have crowded into these once happy homes and transformed them into caravansaries. The mill agents no longer control or supervise these houses to any great extent; the 'corporation streets', once well cared for, have no master and have become the dumping-ground for the refuse of a teeming population. The Greeks crowd the French-Canadians; the French-Canadians, the Irish; the Irish, the native Americans; each earlier race giving way before the lower standard of living of the later.

"The profits of the textile corporations flow largely into the pockets of absentee landlords, and the wages of the employees, after supplying the barest necessities, go in foreign remittances to the friends across the sea."

The happy relationship of the past has been destroyed by several factors. In the first place, as Doctor Kenngott observes, the ownership has passed into the hands of a new generation of absentee owners. What is even more vital, they have adopted a false philosophy of life. They are more interested in the things that money will buy than in the work that is the source of the money. The larger wealth of the owners enables them to consume on a scale that is impossible to the laborers. This tends to separate them into social classes. To counteract this, there is no longer a common interest in a common work to furnish a basis for a common social life with mutual respect and sympathy. This change of interest on the part of the employing class has been encouraged by foreign influences. One of the most common criticisms of American life by foreigners is directed at the propensity of Americans to work when it is no longer necessary. They wonder why we do not stop working and begin to "live", as they call it. They have, some of them, even felt called upon to act as missionaries to win us away from the work-bench philosophy of life and convert us to the pig-trough philosophy; that is, from that philosophy of life which finds the principal field for self-expression in production to that philosophy of life which finds its chief field for self-expression in elegant leisure, graceful consumption and other forms of "conspicuous waste."

In "The Americanization of Edward Bok" [1] we read:

A man can live a life full-square only when he divides it into three periods:

First: that of education, acquiring the fullest and best within his reach and power;

Second: that of achievement: achieving for himself and his family, and discharging the first duty of any man, that in case of his incapacity those who

[1] By Edward W. Bok. Charles Scribner's Sons. New York, 1920.

are closest to him are provided for. But such provision does not mean an accumulation that becomes to those he leaves behind him an embarrassment rather than a protection. To prevent this, the next period confronts him:

Third: Service for others. That is the acid test where many a man falls short: to know when he has enough, and to be willing not only to let well enough alone, but to give a helping hand to the other fellow; to recognize, in a practical way, that we are our brother's keeper; that a brotherhood of man does exist outside after-dinner speeches. Too many men make the mistake, when they reach the point of enough, of going on pursuing the same old game: accumulating more money, grasping for more power until either a nervous breakdown overtakes them and a sad incapacity results, or they drop "in the harness", which is, of course, only calling an early grave by another name. They cannot seem to get the truth into their heads that as they have been helped by others so should they now help others: as their means have come from the public, so now they owe something in turn to that public.

Here Mr. Bok gives expression to a feeling which is not strictly American, for it is more prevalent in old and decadent countries than here, that the period of achievement is not also a period of service.[1] It is, unfortunately, still true that a great

[1] The same foreign idea is expressed in an article by Mr. Bok in the *World's Work* for November, 1924.

many people think that one cannot perform service unless he stops his regular work and begins to do something else. If a man is engaged in honest business, it is a service to the public to have that business conducted in the best possible manner, to have it expand and flourish. Generally the man does more good when he sticks to that kind of business than when he stops and tries to do good in some other way.

We are familiar with the old remark to the effect that he who makes two blades of grass grow where one grew before is doing more good than all the politicians put together. A modern economist would add the words "and than all the social service experts put together." Of course, if a man is engaged in a dishonest business in which he is extracting money from other people without rendering a service or giving them anything that is of any use to them, he is not in any sense a servant. The sooner he quits the better it is for everybody else. But if he is really giving people the equivalent of all the money he gets from them, he is their servant and is entitled to what he gets. In fact, he is entitled to what he gets only because he is their servant.

The spread through this country of the notion that the way to enjoy life, or even to perform service, is to stop one's regular work in which one has developed some expertness and turn to something more elegant or leisurely, is one of the factors which tend to create a gap between those who have to work and those who are able to stop working and enjoy elegant leisure. Another factor that has tended to widen still further the gap is found in the fact that more and more, in the last generation or so, the wage workers have been largely immigrants. There has been very little in the way of a common interest to unite them and their employers. Their habits of living are different, their schooling has been different, their religion has been different, their language and all their traditions are different. It would have been very difficult indeed for the employers and employees to have preserved, under these conditions, the feeling of solidarity that once existed, when the population was homogeneous.

These two factors combined, namely, the shifting of the interest from production to consumption on the part of the inheritors of wealth, and the wide divergence of habits of life between the native-born who supply most of the employers, and the foreign-born who supply most of the employees, created temporarily in this country, on our democratic soil, a class consciousness quite as definite, but fortunately not so deep-seated or permanent as any that existed in older countries with their hereditary notions of class, and their antiquated notions of self-expression. With the restriction of immigration, one of these factors will tend to disappear. After three or four generations of restricted immigration, it will no longer be true that there is a difference of language, education, religion, standard of living or anything else to separate employer from employee. The one uncertain factor is the philosophy of life which is to prevail in this country. If we can preserve the old democratic, robust interest in work rather than in leisure, in production rather than in consumption, this factor in the development of class consciousness will also disappear and with it will disappear the last vestige of class consciousness. With class consciousness will disappear also what we now know as the labor problem. Even the wage question will tend also to disappear through the general tendency toward the equalization of wealth, first through the rise in wages, and second through the reduction of profits and the rate of interest.

III

It is sometimes contended that the immigration of manual laborers from other countries does not produce class consciousness as between employers and employees. As evidence, the fact is cited that some of the bitterest and most militant labor agitators are native-born Americans. This fact, however, is easily accounted for on two grounds. First and least important, there is the fact that wherever discontent exists, some one is likely to be found who will organize that discontent and become its leader and spokesman. The probability in this case is similar to the probability that where an economic demand exists somebody is likely to discover it and take measures to supply it. In many cases the person most competent to organize and give expression to the discontent of these foreign-born laborers is a native American. The more important factor, however, is one that lies deeper. It is difficult to define, but it can be described by means of several illustrations.

We sometimes find among the foreign-born laborers men and women of education and taste. They have been accustomed in their own countries to more appreciation and better treatment than has commonly, in those countries, been awarded to unskilled manual workers. They have belonged to a higher social caste; they have been able to associate with other people of education, culture, and taste. They expect the same appreciation in this country. That is, they expect to be able to associate with the educated and cultured rather than with the uneducated and the unskilled, but there is always difficulty in achieving this ambition in a new country whose language is strange and whose ways are not yet fully understood. Therefore it not infrequently happens that these persons of education are classed with other immigrants and forced to seek their society among the uneducated and unskilled immigrant laborers. They very naturally resent this and become embittered. Some of the most implacable enemies of our economic and social system are for this reason found among these educated immigrants. This is only one illustration of a social principle of wide application.

This situation is similar in kind to many others that we have among us at all times. In the old South where a great deal of unskilled manual work was done by negro slaves, it sometimes happened that white men also were compelled to do unskilled manual work in order to make a living. The mere fact that men have to do unskilled manual work does not in itself produce a sense of social inferiority; but it invariably does produce such a sense if most of that work is done by people who indubitably occupy a lower social status, as did the negro slaves. The free white laborers who had to do the kind of work that was generally done by negro slaves were forced to share something of the social degradation of the negro slaves. Very naturally they resented this most bitterly. In this case, however, their resentment was directed toward the Negro rather than toward the slave owners. The most aggressive enemies of the Negro, have, therefore, always been found among those who have to sell their labor or the products of their labor in competition with Negroes. Even to-day, after slavery has disappeared for more than a generation, the same general attitude of mind survives. The Negroes are still there in large numbers; they occupy a distinctly lower social status, and white laborers who compete with them have to share, in some small degree at least, the social degradation that attaches to negro labor with whom they compete. There has persisted, therefore, a more or less definite distinction between what in the local vernacular is called "niggers' work" and white men's work.

There is nothing in the nature of domestic service to give the domestic servant a lower social status than any other laborer. In our western farming communities of an earlier day, when there were neither negro servants nor immigrant girls, the hired girl and the hired man were not forced into a social class separate from that of the mistress or master. They ate at the same table, rode to church in the same vehicle, went to the same parties, and in all essential respects belonged to the same social class. Under such conditions there was and could have been no class consciousness to separate employers and employees, and consequently there could have been no labor problem, though there might have been endless bickerings over the question of wages.

In the South, however, where most of the domestic service is performed by negro women, it is very difficult, even down to this day, to get white girls to do this kind of work. If large numbers of them were forced into this kind of work in order to get a living, we could expect, with a feeling of absolute certainty, that a definite class consciousness would develop. Servants, even white servants, would be excluded from the social life of the employing class. In this case it would be the existence of negro servants that would produce class consciousness, though once produced, class consciousness would not be confined to negro servants; it would extend to white servants as well. Even in the North, especially the eastern half of the North, most of the domestic service is now performed by immigrant girls. A certain class distinction has grown up, but it is not primarily because of the nature of household service. It is primarily because mistress and servant have so few things in common. Language, religion, habits of life, historical and social background, are all so different that it would be difficult for the two to find a common interest strong enough to unite them or to enable them to share in a common social life.

These observations apply to the labor problem in general. The social conditions in the New England factory towns described by Lucy Larcom and Doctor Kenngott are sufficient to prove that the mere employer-employee relationship is not enough, in and of itself, to produce class distinction. Employer and employee may and frequently do associate on a basis of equality and mutual sympathy and understanding, but it is only where they have common interests, and where no difference of color, race, language, religion, or historical background is thrust between them. But since the factory towns began to be filled with foreign-born workers, shortly after the Civil

War, it has become increasingly true that the great mass of the employers were American born and the great mass of the manual workers were foreign born. This drove a wedge between the two classes, in spite of all our democratic ideals and institutions. While the mass of the manual workers have been foreign born, there have been large numbers of native-born Americans who have been forced to make their living by manual work. These native-born Americans have been classified with other manual workers rather than with their native-born employers. How persistent this tendency to social stratification becomes, when most of the manual workers are foreign born and most of the employers native born, is well illustrated in an illuminating book entitled "One Way Out." [1] This is the story of an American family of some education and culture whose head was not very successful in holding what is commonly known as a white-collar job. The family had become impoverished, and found itself in a condition of real economic distress. The head of the family found, however, that by accepting a definitely lower social status and taking the kind of job ordinarily held by immigrants, he could get good wages and live comfortably. The family merely exchanged a higher social status with poverty for a lower social status with comfort. They even found a comradeship and a social life in the new situation that were quite as

[1] By "William Carleton." Small, Maynard & Company. Boston, 1911.

agreeable as those which they had sacrificed, which meant that the difference between a so-called "higher" and a "lower" social status is almost entirely imaginary.

This difference in social status, however, adds the irritating factor to the wage question that transforms it into what is known as a labor problem. Why, it may be asked, do countries without immigrants have a labor problem? The answer is very clear and simple. These older countries have antiquated, aristocratic traditions that we did not have in this country until we began to import them from abroad.

Even in England, with all its political democracy, the tradition that separates class from class is still a power and it will take several more generations of political democracy to achieve complete social democracy, that is, the absence of any feeling of class distinction. Even to this day, the Englishman's idea of a solution of the labor problem, unless he be himself a laborer, or some sort of a radical, is some device, plan, or policy that will keep the laboring classes satisfied with low wages. The ideal of all sound Americans, however, is that there is no solution of the labor problem until, first, wages are so high as to offer no ground for discontent or dissatisfaction among the wage workers, and, second, there is no class consciousness or feeling of class distinction to be a cause of irritation; in short, when we shall no longer speak of the laboring "classes."

This is now in process of being achieved. Laborers are rapidly becoming capitalists as well as laborers; and to a gradually increasing degree, capitalists are finding it difficult to hire all their work done and are compelled to do more and more of it themselves. In short, capitalists are becoming laborers as well as capitalists. This actual blending of the two so-called classes means that there will be no more classes in this country. Fraternity has never been very clearly defined, but this condition, when there is no class consciousness, comes as near being fraternity as we are ever likely to get, if it be not fraternity itself.

CHAPTER FOUR

The Growing Financial Power of Laborers

I

THERE are at least three kinds of evidence to indicate that American laborers are growing rapidly in financial power. First, we have the statistics regarding the old-time forms of thrift such as savings deposits, the assets of building and loan associations, and the premiums paid to insurance companies.[1] In addition to these we have some incomplete but rather striking figures regarding the investment of laboring people in the stocks and bonds of corporations. Finally, we have the new phenomenon of the labor bank.

Now, even though there should be a phenomenal growth in the financial power of labor, it does not necessarily follow that savings deposits should increase proportionally. This for two reasons, that savings deposits are essentially in the nature of nest eggs or small funds for meeting unlooked-for emergencies, and besides, no matter how prosperous a person becomes, he is not likely to add greatly to his savings: most of his surplus being

[1] *See* article by the author in the *Financial World*, May 31, 1924; also one in *Aera*, October, 1924.

turned to other things. But what we might expect is a relative decline in savings, as investments in stocks and bonds and deposits in labor banks might be accounted for partly by withdrawals from savings deposits. Such figures as we have, however, show clearly that there has been no depletion in savings deposits, but some increase.

This remark is made to anticipate two possible objections, first, that the decline in the purchasing power of the dollar should, in itself, have led to a doubling of savings deposits in order to put the depositors in the same economic position as they were during pre-war days; and second, that the normal increase in population should have resulted in some increase in total savings. The figures for savings deposits, however, show that the increase is more than sufficient to balance the increase in population and the decline in the purchasing power of the dollar. In other words, the increase in the investments in stocks and bonds and in the shares and deposits of labor banks have not been made by reducing savings deposits even proportionally.

As to savings deposits, the following figures,[1] published by the Savings Bank Division of the American Bankers Association, are significant. They include the total savings deposits in five classes of banks, the per capita deposits, and the number

[1] *See* "Savings Deposits and Depositors" for the years 1912 through 1924, compiled and published by Savings Bank Division, American Bankers Association, New York.

of depositors for 1914 and 1924. The five classes of banks are mutual savings, State banks, trust companies, private banks, and national banks.

Year	Total Savings Deposits	Per Capita Savings Deposits	Total Number Savings Depositors
1914	$8,728,536,000	$89	11,385,734
1924	20,873,562,000	186	38,867,994

These figures show that the total savings deposits have considerably more than doubled in ten years. The per capita savings have slightly more than doubled, whereas the total number of depositors has increased more than three-fold. Of course, not all savings are made by wage workers, but the rather phenomenal increase in the total number of savers indicates that a very large number of small savers have been added in ten years. There is a reasonable probability that wage workers furnish a fair share of these small savers.

As to the vast fund of life insurance owned by the patrons of the great life insurance companies, it is well known that the most phenomenal growth in the whole insurance business has been in those companies that specialize in industrial insurance. According to Richard Boeckel[1] more than two-thirds of the life insurance policies at present (1924) in force in this country are held by wage workers. This does not state how the volume of insurance held by them compares with that held by other people. In 1912

[1] *See* the *Forum*, April, 1924.

the total insurance in force was approximately fifteen and a half billion dollars. Mr. David F. Houston, Ex-Secretary of the Treasury, estimates[1] that there are outstanding at the present time (January, 1925) in the neighborhood of eighty-three million insurance policies for more than sixty billion dollars. This represents, in terms of dollars, though not, of course, in purchasing power, almost a five-fold increase since 1912. The total amount is greater, in terms of dollars, than the pre-war wealth of France and nearly as great as the estimated wealth of this country in 1890. Since the holders of these insurance policies are really the owners of the property in which insurance funds are invested, there are about forty-five million owners who hold this form of property.

When we consider the assets of building and loan associations, we find that they are increasing at about the same rate as savings deposits. The following figures show their growth.

Year	Total Membership	Total Assets
1914	3,103,935	$1,357,707,900
1923	7,202,880	3,940,939,880

During the year 1923 alone there were paid into the life insurance companies $2,427,327,961. This sum represents the savings of a given year. How much the present holders of life insurance policies have actually paid into the insurance companies is not recorded, but some of these policies of course

[1] *See* the *World's Work,* January, 1925.

have been running for many years, some for only a few years. It would seem reasonable to assume that they have run on the average approximately five years. If we add together the total payments to life insurance companies during the last five years we get the sum of $9,852,127,693. Adding this to the total savings deposits for 1924 and the total assets of building and loan associations for 1923, we get the enormous sum of $34,666,629,573. Of course this must be discounted somewhat because these savings are not wholly by laboring people. Discount this as much as we dare, it is still a fair inference that the share of working people in the billions of savings will be somewhere in the billions. Any day the laborers decide to do so, they can divert a few billions of savings to the purchase of the common stock of industrial corporations, railroads, and public service companies, and actually control considerable numbers of them. This is not necessarily a good policy, but it is within their power to do so if they decide that it is to their interest.

A number of independent inquiries have shown a great increase in the number of investors in the shares of corporations. It is well to be on our guard, however, lest we infer too much as to the wide diffusion of corporate ownership. Even though there were no increase in the total number of investors, if each investor scattered his investments, the result would be that the shareholders of any individual corporation would show an increase in number. That is to say, if at any one time there were ten large investors in the shares of Corporation A, ten in the shares of Corporation B, ten in the shares of Corporation C, whereas a little later, these same thirty investors decide to spread their investments, each investing equally in the shares of all three corporations, the figures would show that, whereas formerly there were ten investors in the shares of each corporation, now there are thirty. From this a superficial observer might infer that a wide diffusion of the ownership of corporations in general had taken place. There is, however, sufficient evidence to show that the apparent diffusion of ownership of our great corporations is not simply apparent but real. A considerable number of large corporations show that thousands of wage workers are becoming owners who were never corporate owners before. There are other lines of evidence to show that many non-wage workers are investing in the shares of corporations who never before did anything of the kind.

As to the investment of laboring people in the shares of corporations, some interesting figures are available, though the half has not yet been told. The *Financial World* sent a questionnaire in March, 1924, to 1000 of the leading corporations of the country for the purpose of finding out how far the movement had progressed. Only 129 replies were returned. Of these 104 showed that employees below the grade of officials owned stock, though

118 of the replies stated that the management favored the plan. Of those that showed employee ownership, only 54 had offered special inducements to persuade employees to buy stock. What are known as public utility corporations showed the strongest tendency toward the plan.

The largest number of employee stockholders in any single industrial corporation that answered the questionnaire was 50,020, owning 689,703 shares. Two others show 15,000 employee stockholders each, owning in one case 450,411 shares and 200,000 in the other. One smaller corporation reports that all its common stock is owned by its employees, but does not tell how it is distributed between the official class and the manual workers. Another reports that 12,000 of its 18,000 employees own stock. Still another reports that 3,000 of its 6,000 employees own $2,500,000 worth of stock. A number of corporations that did not reply to the questionnaire are known to have a considerable number of employee stockholders.

Of the 171 public utility corporations listed, 33 replies were received, 32 of which report employee stockholders. One reports that 94 per cent. of its employees own from 1 to 50 shares each; another that 149 of its 151 employees own stock; still another that 510 of its 543 employees own 5,211 shares. The most striking case, however, is a well-known traction company, all of whose 11,500 employees own stock amounting to 120,000 shares. One company reports that none but officers own stock.

Among those that did not reply to the questionnaire, the Southwestern Bell Telephone Company has published in its annual report the statement that

> The Employees' Stock Purchase Plan, under which employees may subscribe for capital stock of the American Telephone and Telegraph Company on favorable terms continues in effect. On December 31, 1923, more than 5,900 employees were subscribing for 17,496 shares. Since the introduction of the existing Plan in May, 1921, more than 14,000 employees have exercised their privilege of participation and a large percentage of employees of the Company already are shareholders of record. The Plan provides not only a means for acquiring a high-grade investment stock but as well a means for promoting systematic saving.

A report on Employees' Thrift and Savings Plans, prepared by The Policyholders' Service Bureau of the Metropolitan Life Insurance Company,[1] mentions a number of other companies in which the plan is in operation, in one of which — a large motor company — ninety-four per cent. of the employees are participating in the plan for employee stock ownership. In a large soap manufacturing company, sixty to eighty-five per cent. of the employees own $1,600,000 worth of stock. This report shows that a consider-

[1] August, 1921.

able number of companies that did not reply to the questionnaire of the *Financial World* are making use of this plan.

There is furthermore a report prepared by the Metropolitan Life Insurance Company based on a study of the practice of a number of companies that have developed such plans. The report is not a brief for or against employee stock ownership, but merely aims to describe the plans that are in actual operation. It finds three principal types: first, where the cost is borne entirely by the employee; second, where the cost is borne jointly by the company and the employee; third, where the stock is given to the employee. The report closes with a chart giving the names of the companies of each type that were studied.

The majority of those studied belong to type one. This group includes not only more individual companies but larger companies than either of the others. It includes, for example, the United States Steel Corporation, Swift and Company, the General Electric Company, the Ford Motor Company, the American Telephone and Telegraph Company, and fourteen others. The companies listed under type two include such well-known corporations as the General Motors, the Standard Oil Company of Indiana, the Studebaker Corporation, the Statler Hotels Corporation, and others. As would be expected, there are certain rather definite conditions imposed by the company that pays a part of the cost of the stock. Under type three are listed the Dennison Manufacturing Company, the International Harvester Company, the John B. Stetson Company, and several others. In these cases, where the stock is given to the employees, it is uniformly on the basis of length of service or for meritorious service. The result of plans now in operation, as shown in the following quotation, is interesting: [1]

One of the few tangible measures is the percentage of employee stockholders to the total number of employees. This shows a wide variation but is relatively higher in the smaller companies. The percentages range from five per cent. to as high as eighty-five per cent. with an average for the larger companies in the neighborhood of twenty-two per cent. The following summary shows the number of employees subscribing to stock of the United States Steel Corporation over a period of seven years, the average number of employees, the number of shares subscribed for, and the percentage of employees who were shareholders during those years:

	1916	1917	1918	1919	1920	1921	1922
No. of Employees. . .	252,668	268,058	268,710	252,106	267,345	191,700	214,931
No. of Employee Subscribers . .	25,143	39,252	43,777	61,324	66,311	81,722	34,009
Percentage . .	10	14	16	24	25	42	16
No. of Shares Purchased .	50,269	67,752	96,645	158,061	167,263	255,325	93,645

[1] *See* "A Report on Employee Stock-Ownership Plans", page 9, published by the Metropolitan Life Insurance Company. New York.

Some idea of the rate of growth of employee ownership in this corporation is shown by the fact that in 1902, out of a total of 43,019 stockholders, 27,379 were employees, whereas in March, 1924, out of a total of 159,000 stockholders, 50,020 were employees. This shows more than a trebling of the total number of stockholders and almost a doubling of the number of employee owners.

In the chapter on The Workman as Stockholder in "Labor's Money", by Richard Boeckel;[1] the following information is given:

Twenty-one thousand of the employees of Swift and Company, constituting more than one-third of the total number of men and women employed by the company, hold Swift shares with a total par value exceeding $21,000,000.

Ninety-four thousand of the employees of the American Telephone and Telegraph Company are making payment in installments upon stocks subscribed under the company's profit sharing plan. Of this number approximately 46,000 hold shares upon which payment has been made in full.

The E. I. du Pont de Nemours Company has distributed stock valued at $20,765,999 among its employees since the inauguration of its plan. The total distribution in 1923 amounted to 14,484 shares with a total par value of $1,448,400.

Six thousand employees of the General Motors Corporation, one out of every twelve employed, hold

[1] Harcourt, Brace & Company. New York, 1923.

270,000 shares of common stock in that corporation, valued in excess of $4,000,000.

Employees of Sears, Roebuck and Company own 55,700 shares in that enterprise, purchased through the employees' profit sharing fund, and 77,600 shares purchased outside the fund.

Seventy per cent. of the workers employed by the International Harvester Company hold common stock in the company, the aggregate value of their holdings exceeding $5,000,000.

Practically every workman employed by the Procter & Gamble Company is a shareholder in the enterprise. Ninety per cent. of the employees of the Firestone Tire and Rubber Company are stockholders. Every third man in the employ of the Goodyear Tire and Rubber Company holds one or more shares of stock.

The United States Steel Corporation, called by Samuel Untermyer "the greatest enemy to industrial peace in America", was a pioneer in employees' stock distribution. The corporation was chartered in 1901. Its stock subscription plan was put into operation in 1903. In every year but one since 1903 the corporation has offered large amounts of its stock, bought in the open market, for subscription by its employees. In the beginning only preferred stock was offered, but offerings since 1916 have all been of common stock. Employees are allowed three years in which to pay for stock subscribed. An annual bonus of $5, in addition to the regular dividends, is paid to each employee holding his stock for a period of five years.

In recent years all the corporation's offerings to employees have been largely over-subscribed.

Ex-Secretary Houston [1] finds still further evidence of a rapid growth in the number of stockholders in the leading corporations.

In 1911 there were 6,078 stockholders of the Standard Oil Company of New Jersey, whereas in 1924 there were 300,000. Armour and Company was formerly largely a family affair; in 1924 there were 77,000 shareholders. There are 46,751 stockholders of Swift & Company. Of the total of 123,751 owners of these two companies, 55,000, or nearly half, were reported to be employees.

Ten representative retail trade corporations, with total sales of just under one billion dollars, report 8,323,762 shares of stock with a total value of more than $376,700,000 and 40,767 stockholders. One of these companies reports employee holdings of 133,000 shares.

The Bethlehem Steel Company reports 49,497 stockholders with 14,000 employees subscribing for shares under their present plan.

In 1890 there were 81,252 stockholders of thirty-three railroads, with average holdings of $17,087. By 1923 the number of stockholders had risen to 602,000, and the average stock per stockholder had fallen more than forty per cent. Of the Class I

[1] *See ante*, page 93.

American railroads there were in 1923 over 800,000 owners, with an average holding of $9,319.

In the electric light and power industry there were a million and a quarter owners in 1923. It is estimated that owners of all the gas, electric railway, light and power utilities now (January, 1925) exceed two million in number. One hundred and eighty-five companies report to the National Electric Light Association that their customer owner campaigns from 1914 to 1923 have secured 652,900 stockholders. Fifty-six of these companies reported that thirty-eight per cent. of their employees were stockholders. The American Gas Association states that 187 companies sold an average of 5½ shares to 227,170 customers in twenty months. The Commonwealth Edison Company had 11 stockholders in 1883, and 34,256 in 1923. The Pacific Gas and Electric Company in 1914 had 4,128 holders, in 1923, 26,291. The Southern California Edison had 2,000 stockholders in 1917; in 1923, 65,636. The Standard Gas and Electric Company reports that seventy-five per cent. of the employees are stockholders; the Northern States Power Company that eighty per cent. of its employees are stockholders.

The Western Union Telegraph Company had 1,382 stockholders in 1875, with an average of about 244 shares. In 1923 the number of stockholders had increased to 26,276, with an average holding of 38 shares. In 1900 the American Telephone and Telegraph Company had 7,535 stockholders; in 1924 they had more than 343,000, with an average of 26 shares. Sixty-five thousand of the employees of the Bell System are stockholders.

It is impossible to account for all this vast increase in the number of shareholders by assuming that a limited number of large shareholders are scattering their investments. Many thousands of employee and customer owners are practically all new owners. Out of a total of 60,000 employees of Armour and Company, some 40,000 are stockholders in that company (December 27, 1924). There are also other evidences, as will be shown, to the effect that large numbers of people who never before invested in the shares of corporations are now doing so.

In the article already referred to, Mr. Houston presents some interesting figures as to the occupational classification of purchasers of the preferred stock offered by the Bell Telephone Company of Pennsylvania, the Wisconsin Telephone Company and the Southwestern Bell Telephone Company. Probably every occupation is represented. The largest number of subscribers is classified as laborers, the second largest as housewives, though the housewives lead in the number of shares with 132,042 shares, laborers come second with 82,182 shares, manufacturers third with 53,366 shares, and clerks fourth with 44,060 shares.

One of the most interesting and comprehensive

plans for employee ownership is that put in operation by the Philadelphia Rapid Transit Company. This plan became effective January 1, 1922, and has since been continued.[1] To begin with, there is a basic wage rate at the present time (1924). This is based on the average of wages prevailing in three cities — Chicago, Detroit, and Cleveland — under a plan originally adopted as a wartime expedient. The maximum surface trainman's wage is made the base, and when this wage is changed, wages in all other departments are adjusted accordingly.

The present (1924) wages of the Philadelphia Rapid Transit trainmen are as follows:

	RATES PER HOUR		
	New Men	After 3 Months	After 1 Year
Surface motormen and conductors	60¢	63¢	65¢
One-man car operators	65	68	70
Elevated motormen	63	66	68
Elevated conductors	60	63	65
Elevated guards	60	62	63

In addition to these wages the employees receive a wage dividend not to exceed ten per cent. of the annual payroll, provided they earn that amount by added effort, after a six per cent. dividend has been paid to stockholders. This wage dividend is not paid in cash, but is kept intact in a coöperative wage dividend fund. This fund is being used by the employees to purchase stock in the company. At the

[1] *See* pamphlet entitled "A Bird's-Eye View of P.R.T.", published by the Philadelphia Rapid Transit Company, Philadelphia, September 1, 1924.

beginning of 1924 the workers had purchased and held under complete ownership 120,000 shares of Philadelphia Rapid Transit Stock with a market value of $4,200,000. This is one-fifth of the entire issue of stock. In February, 1925, 11,000 employees held $10,300,000 worth of common stock of this company. This fund and the stock purchased with it are held and administered by trustees elected by the employees. The voting power of the stock is also lodged in the trustees.

In case of the death of the employee, or in the event of his leaving the service, provision is made either for cash payment of his deposits in the fund, or delivery of the shares held in his account. The decision as to whether cash or stock shall be paid rests with the trustees.

In addition to the $4,200,000 worth of stock in the company that employs them, the employees also have a coöperative savings fund on which they receive five per cent. interest. This rate is made possible by the purchase of large blocks of securities during the post-war period when interest rates were high and the price of securities low. There are now 9,288 members with deposits of over $2,000,000. This savings fund, like the wage dividend fund, is administered by trustees who are elected by the employees. The trustees make their investments with competent banking advice. The following table shows their investments at the close of 1923:

U. S. Government & Fed'l Land Bank Bonds .	$253,650.00
Canadian Bonds	25,000.00
Real Estate Mortgages	50,000.00
Steam Railroad Bonds	570,000.00
Equipment Trust Certificates	422,000.00
Public Utility Bonds	736,000.00
Total Par Value	$2,056,650.00
As Charged on Books	$2,019,619.73

In an excellent article on "The Distribution of Corporate Ownership in the United States"[1] by H. T. Warshow, the author concludes that there has been an increase from about 4,400,000 stockholders in 1900 to about 14,400,000 in 1922, or about 250 per cent. There has been, furthermore, a shifting of ownership from the "wealthy few" to the "middle" and "wage-earning" classes. This conclusion is based on a careful study of several lines of evidence. The author mentions particularly: (1) "The division of ownership of corporations, as manifested by the number of stockholders and the average number of shares held by each stockholder, obtained by questionnaires and published statements.

(2) "The amount of dividends received by the various income classes in the United States as revealed by income-tax statistics. These two avenues, although independently traversed, lead to the same conclusions."

The increase in the number of stockholders, noted above, and the shifting of the ownership of corpora-

[1] For elaborate tables, on which Mr. Warshow bases these conclusions, *see* the *Quarterly Journal of Economics*, for November, 1924.

tions from the wealthier classes to those of moderate and small means, is evidenced by several facts. "In 1921, for example, the income-tax figures show that the classes in the United States with incomes under $20,000 per annum received 53.2 per cent. of the dividends paid, which means that the class receiving incomes of over $20,000 per annum had an equity of less than fifty per cent. in the corporations of the United States." To quote at length from Mr. Warshow's able article:

1. For the income class of over $20,000, the largest aggregate, both in absolute figures and in percentage of total dividends received, is found in 1916 and amounts to $1,694,000,000 or 79.3 per cent. of the total dividends reported. This is followed by practically an uninterrupted decrease in the percentages of dividends reported by this class each year until 1921, when the lowest figure — $1,158,000,000, equal to 46.8 per cent. of total dividends — is reached. The year 1922 shows a slight increase over 1921, but remains lower than any of the other years.

2. The dividends received by the class of $5,000 to $10,000 show a large increase from 1916 to 1917 and a further increase from 1917 to 1918. From then on, the dividends received by this class are comparatively stable both in absolute amount and in percentage of the total dividends reported. . . .

The largest increase occurs in the class of incomes of $1,000 to $5,000. In 1916, the dividends received by this group amount to only $38,000,000 or 1.8 per cent. of the total dividends reported. The figures for this year, as was pointed out above, should not be used for comparative purposes, since the exemption limits were so high in 1916 as to make the number of returns in this class small. The year 1917, therefore, should be the first year for comparative purposes. In 1917, dividends reported by this class amounted to $190,000,000 or 9.5 per cent. of the total dividends reported. In 1918, this amount rose to $335,000,000 or 14.1 per cent. of the total. In 1919, there was a drop of about ten million dollars in the total amount and a decrease to 13.3 per cent. In 1920, there was a rise to $372,000,000. The year 1921, however, marked the point of greatest increase, rising to $562,000,000 or 22.7 per cent. of the total dividends reported. In 1922, there was a slight decrease from the high point of 1921, but it still remained at $491,000,000, which is higher than any previous year except 1921.

To summarize. The figures demonstrate that since 1916 there has been an increase in the aggregate amount of annual dividends paid by corporations in the United States. Both the absolute and proportionate shares of this total, which go to the class of income above $20,000 (to be designated for the purposes of this paper the "wealthy" group of the country) show substantial decreases from year to year over the period 1916 to 1921. The group which may here be termed the "middle class", whose income ranges from $5,000 to $20,000, shows moderate increases in the amount of annual dividends received for the period 1916 to 1921, both in absolute figures and in proportion to the total. The largest and most significant increase in dividends received has taken place in the class of incomes below $5,000 per annum, in the group which includes the "wage-earning class."

In the *United States Investor* of October 11, 1924, Mr. Dwight W. Morrow of J. P. Morgan and Company presents a paper entitled "The Investor." Among other things he considers the wide distribution of certain recent investments, particularly the Austrian and the Japanese loans. Inquiries had been made of twenty-three banking houses that acted as distributors for these bonds. These twenty-three houses were widely scattered geographically and represented different classes of investors. The twenty-three houses had 2,970 customers who bought Austrian bonds. The average investment per customer was $2,980. Extending the figures to the entire country, he estimated that the bonds were taken by about nine thousand American investors. The same twenty-three had 8,212 customers who bought Japanese bonds. The average investment of these customers was $2,680. On the basis of these figures, he estimates that the entire Japanese loan was purchased by approximately forty-four thousand investors. These facts indicate a tendency on the part of small investors to increase in numbers and in the quantity of their investments. Further analysis shows that approximately fifty per cent. of the number of sales of both Austrian and Japanese bonds were made to persons who invested a thousand dollars or less. Approximately ninety per cent. of the number of sales — not of the aggregate — were to investors whose purchases were limited to five thousand dollars or less. Only about four per cent. of the total number of sales were for amounts over ten thousand dollars.

Putting the classification on the basis of the aggregate amount subscribed, the small investor and the larger seem to be about equal. The sales to persons who invested no more than a thousand dollars accounted for the absorption of only fifteen per cent. of the entire amount of the Austrian bonds and ten per cent. of the Japanese. If, says he, the limit is raised to include all the sales not exceeding five thousand dollars, we find that the persons in this group accounted for sixty-two per cent. of the amount furnished Austria and forty-four per cent. of the amount furnished Japan. Taking the two loans together, approximately ninety per cent. of the investors took about fifty per cent. of the loans.

The tabulation of these twenty-three houses indicated something else. Nearly four hundred persons who had from one hundred to four hundred dollars in savings to spare, took that money and bought Austrian bonds. Nearly three thousand more of the small investors bought Japanese bonds.

These and other figures presented show clearly

enough that the sum total of investments by small investors, presumably in the wage-working class, is only a small percentage of the total investments of the country. They are obviously a long way from getting control of the industries of the country through their investments. That, however, is not the important point. As already stated, the significant thing is that they have money to invest, and are actually investing in increasing numbers, thus becoming small capitalists and getting a share of whatever profits are made by larger investors.

These figures also show what could be done in specific industries if all the workers chose to invest all their savings in the shares of existing corporations. They do not show that it would be wise for them to do so. It cannot be too often repeated that in this democratic country laborers are exactly like everybody else, and are entitled to the same advice as well as to the same opportunities. There is no better reason for advising a laborer who happens to work for a given corporation to invest in its shares than there would be for advising anybody else to do so. If the investment is in itself suitable for people with small savings, the laborer who happens to work for that corporation may as well invest in its shares as in any other. If that corporation has not yet reached that stage of stability and solvency which makes its shares suitable investments for small investors, the fact that a laborer happens to work for it should not be cited as a reason why he should invest his money there.

II

In addition to the accumulation of savings by working people and the investment in the stock of corporations we have in this country a strikingly new phenomenon in the form of the labor bank. The general facts regarding them, as they existed at the time, are well stated in "Labor's Money" by Richard Boeckel. A more recent statement by the same author appears in *Public Affairs* for November, 1924. He states that the first labor bank in the United States was established at Washington, D. C., in 1920, and that six months later, the Brotherhood of Locomotive Engineers opened a bank in Cleveland. In 1921 two more labor banks were opened, five were opened in 1922, eight in 1923, and sixteen in 1924 up to November, making thirty-three in all. Plans were under way for twenty more when he wrote the above, with a prospect that forty may be in operation by the close of 1924 and seventy-five by the end of 1925.

It is apparent that the movement is proceeding so rapidly that any figures will be out of date before they can be published. The movement has developed far enough to have its own organ, the *Labor Banker*, a well-edited and prosperous-looking journal. Its editorials and articles compare favorably with those of other financial journals, and it shows, on the whole, a practical common sense worthy of students of Benjamin Franklin.

In the *World's Work* for November, 1924, is an article on "Labor's Chain of Banks" by Warren S. Stone, president of the Brotherhood of Locomotive Engineers. This organization has been most active in the field of labor banking and has more banks than any other single organization. Mr. Stone declares that the growth of the movement has been amazing and that, by the end of the year 1924, the combined resources of the labor banks in the United States will be in the neighborhood of $150,000,000; that the Brotherhood of Locomotive Engineers will have twelve in operation (there are ten in November); and the total will be more than thirty. As he writes, he declares that seven more are in process of formation, and that there are sixty applications on his desk, asking how to proceed and awaiting investigation. The organization does not try to hurry the process, but tries rather to keep the brake on it. They do not want any of the new banks to fail, or to fall into the hands of persons not in sympathy with their aims.

He goes on to ask, "What can a labor bank do for labor that any commercial or savings bank or trust company can't do?" "To begin with," he says, "we can make the workingman feel at home." He declares that though he has been going into banks for forty years, he has not got over that chilly feeling which always comes when he enters; whereas any workman who goes into these labor banks knows that he is welcome. He is made to feel easy, even if he is not there to do business.

That the labor banks have been accepted in regular banking circles is evidenced by the cordial relationship existing between their Cleveland bank and the National City Bank. Mr. Stone quotes from Charles E. Mitchell, president of the National City Bank, as follows:

> We think the result will be more savings, more banking business, increased demand for labor, greater prosperity, and an impetus to social progress.
>
> Furthermore, we think the logical tendency from this development of labor banks will be for labor to take a larger part in all kinds of business, and that this will be for the general good. We do not think that the wage-earners should be nothing but employees, but that they should plan to share in ownership. The modern form of corporate organization makes it possible for thousands of persons to participate in the ownership of an industry, either as bondholders or stockholders, and we believe that it will be for the good of the country to have the railroads and larger industries owned in this manner. We do not want a sharp line drawn between the owners and workers, but rather that the two shall be the

same or closely intermingled. The result will be better understanding and more effective coöperation.

Regarding the policy of the labor bank, Mr. Stone says:

The usual savings bank tries to get its depositors to leave their money in its care. It can pay four per cent, say, compounded semi-annually, and still turn the money over at a profit. But we try to get our savings depositors to take their money out. As soon as a man has saved $500 we suggest to him that he put it into a bond. We are trying to get our people into the habit of thrift, for all of us are creatures of habit. Once a man has clipped a coupon for the first time he wants to cut another, and he begins saving to buy another bond.

The Brotherhood of Locomotive Engineers Co-operative National Bank of Cleveland which I am best qualified to discuss here because I happen to be president of it, has an investment department which keeps an eye open for the kind of bonds it can recommend to our customers. We demand that they shall be good investments. Working people who save are always putting their money into investments, like other Americans, for we are an investing nation; but working people heretofore have often put their funds into bad stocks and wildcat schemes. We are trying to stop that. We are trying to educate them into safe markets.

The first time our Cleveland bank joined the biggest Wall Street bank in a bond purchase marked

an epoch in American finance. It was historic, not on account of the sum involved, but on account of the nature of the joint investors. The Cleveland bank and the National City Company, which is a subsidiary of the billion-dollar National City Bank, took over together $3,500,000 bonds of the International Great Northern Railroad Company, at a price to yield about 6.35 per cent. to the investor. It was not an underwriting transaction but a joint purchase. Here was a Wall Street bank joining hands with a labor bank in a financial deal. In the future there will be many more such deals. Their significance cannot be overestimated.

Now, the Cleveland bank, in marketing those bonds, offered them first to the men employed on the International-Great Northern Railroad. Every locomotive engineer, every fireman, every conductor or mechanic, who bought one of those bonds, had a sudden added interest in the railway. He was a creditor. The first interest of the creditor is in the solvency of the debtor. As the International-Great Northern prospers, so will its bondholders be assured of a good investment. The workers who hold its securities will do their level best to see that it gets and gives good service, because that way prosperity lies.

We think it better for our men to buy bonds than to buy stocks. We like the partnership which stocks confer, but we do not believe that many workmen can afford to assume the risks involved. Bonds bring that sense of responsibility which workingmen ought to have, and they bring a sense of security, if they are good bonds, which stocks seldom give.

Labor banks are tapping a big investment field which has been left heretofore chiefly to the devices of the wildcatter. The Brotherhood has its own insurance, because the old line companies will not insure us at any price; driving an engine is rated as an extra-hazardous occupation, and it is a fact that the average term of insured life after a man comes to us is only eleven years and seven days. So the Brotherhood is paying, into the homes of deceased and disabled locomotive engineers about three millions a year. This goes for the most part into the hands of inexperienced women and perhaps of children, who have been the prey of get-rich-quick swindlers. It is safe to say that nine-tenths of this money has been wasted within a year. We have succeeded in changing this. From the time the Cleveland bank was started we have averaged about a million a month in deposits. This is only one bank. The saving power of American workingmen is so great that, if they would save and carefully invest their savings, *in ten years they could be one of the dominating financial powers of the world.*[1]

Labor banks are not only becoming the reservoirs of money which would be wasted or badly invested otherwise; they are also bringing funds out of the stocking and marmalade jar. Not long ago the actuary of the United States Treasury estimated that there was about $400,000,000 hidden away out of the sight of banks. He seemed to think that this

[1] The italics are the author's.

was just miserliness, but all of us know that the people of this country are more likely to be skeptical and distrustful than miserly. Do you know any one who likes to gloat over the mere sight of paper money, or even gold? I don't. Part at least of this money was in the stocking because the owner feared to trust banks. We have had some ugly failures in this country, and it has upset confidence in that class of our population which knows least about banking. In fact our bankers as a class are distinguished by probity. They are the men we ask to take care of our money — those of us who are educated to banking — and they are the men we ask first to head the subscription list when there is a public movement afoot. But the fact remains that, partly perhaps through ignorance, huge sums are being kept out of banks, where they ought to be.

We found that out as soon as we opened the Cleveland bank. We got deposits not merely from unionized working men and women, but also from professional men and seamstresses and stenographers and clerks. We got deposits from every State in the Union, from the Canal Zone, Central America, Cuba, Germany, Ireland, and Mexico. We have more than 4,000 out-of-town accounts, and less than 1,500 of them are of members of the B. of L. E. We do an immense volume of banking by mail. I cannot but believe that some of this money was concealed in stockings and tin cans until the labor banks began to come into being. And the labor banks will justify the faith thus manifested in them.

Where else in the world is it possible to-day to find such a movement as the rapid multiplication of labor banks in this country? It is too early to say how well they will be managed. In spite of the misgivings that were raised by some demagogic utterances of certain promoters, the actual management seems to have been, so far as an outside observer can tell, sound and conservative. It would not be strange if the practice of the managers and promoters should turn out to be much better than their preaching, since that is almost universally the case with everybody. However, there is no denying the fact that a new-found power is intoxicating and may prove too much of a load for some of the weaker heads to carry. This much at least can be said, and it is really the significant thing: *the American laborers have money to invest.* No amount of preaching will teach them or any other class to invest wisely. They will have to learn, as other people have had to learn, by experience.

Richard M. Boeckel, in the article referred to above, quoted Mr. Peter Brady, the fraternal delegate from the American Federation of Labor to the British Labor Congress, as saying before that Congress that "each year $25,000,000,000 is paid in wages to our industrial workers and from $6,000,000,000 to $7,000,000,000 is saved in various ways. It is this large sum which labor banks hope eventually to control."

Whether these funds are controlled by the labor

banks, by the regular savings banks, by the building and loan associations, by the insurance companies, or whether they are invested by the laborers themselves in the shares of our industrial corporations, it is apparent that they will give to our laborers a considerable degree of control over the industries and the financial institutions of the country.

To a certain extent this diffusion of ownership among laborers, customers, and the general public has been deliberately promoted by corporation managers. To a certain extent, also, it is probably a result of the thrift campaigns that were carried on during and immediately after the Great War. There is, however, no reason for doubting that it is, to a certain extent, a result of the fact that the manual workers have more money available for investment than they used to have. Prohibition may help to account for that. Even if it were wholly the result of stock selling and thrift campaigns, one exceedingly pertinent and consoling remark might be made. These bond-selling campaigns have not, as yet, been very widespread or long continued, but some striking results have already been achieved. The thrift campaigns were brief and not very efficiently staged, and yet there has been a great increase in thrift. If such mild efforts toward the promotion of thrift and investment can produce such striking results, what might not be accomplished by a better organized and more persistent propaganda?

Let us compare this propaganda for economic sanity, and its results, with the floods of radical propaganda in favor of economic insanity. For years our laboring classes have been flooded with radical literature of every tint. Radical doctrines have been dinned into their ears incessantly. Those who were familiar with the extent and the intensity of this propaganda have wondered how a laboring man could ever keep his head, or think in a straight line. That the American working man was not utterly bewildered and demoralized is evidence of his fundamental soundness of heart and mind.

In spite of two generations of incessant propaganda in favor of radicalism, the American laboring men have not become radical. In spite of the efforts of their radical leaders to deliver the labor vote to radical candidates, the radical candidates do not get the labor vote. The propaganda in favor of thrift and investment has not been one tenth or one hundredth part as voluminous or intense as the propaganda of radicalism, and yet it has accomplished greater results in ten years than radicalism has accomplished in fifty years.

"*Sanity* reigns and the government at Washington still lives!"

CHAPTER FIVE

The Financial Policy of Labor

I

IT is true that all these vast sums representing the accumulations of wage workers are a small proportion of the total capital of the country. Moreover, with all their purchases of the shares of corporations, they have not yet acquired a controlling interest in many of our industries. On the other hand, it is not altogether desirable, even from their own point of view, that they should. What the laborers really want, if they know their own interest, is the very best management that can be secured for these industries. It is only by superb management that any industry can expand. The general expansion of all our industries depends upon getting the most superb management that can possibly be secured. If the laborers themselves can secure this, well and good; but it is going rather far to assume that they could, in a very short time, acquire enough knowledge and experience of managerial problems to do this. Meanwhile, in order to give the best advice to laborers one must assume that they are just like other people and do not need advice that differs from what one would give to other would-be investors. That advice would undoubtedly be to invest, all things considered, where there is the best chance of getting something back on the investment. It does not necessarily follow that to acquire a controlling interest in a corporation, even the one that employs him, would give the laborer the best return on his investment.

Nevertheless, it is true that if all the vast sums that have been accumulated and are now being accumulated by American laborers in the form of savings deposits, life-insurance policies, trade-union dues, payments to building and loan associations, and deposits in these labor banks, were invested in the common stock of a few great business corporations, the laboring men could, if they really wanted to, soon own a controlling interest in many of these corporations. It was pointed out, some time ago, in the *Railway Age* [1] and quoted in "Labor's Money" that the employees of the American railways could, in a comparatively short time, acquire a controlling interest in our railroads by the simple device of buying the common stock until they owned more than fifty per cent. of it. It was pointed out that the total par value of the railroad stocks outstanding on December 31, 1917, was $6,583,000,000. If the railway employees would save merely the increase which they had recently received in their wages, it would

[1] *See* article entitled, "Why do not Railway Employees Buy American Railroads", in *Railway Age*, Vol. 69, No. 11, p. 430.

give them $625,000,000 a year for investment. On this basis, if they bought railroad shares at par, they could, by investing all their savings and dividends in railway stocks, buy $3,490,000,000 worth within five years. This would give a substantial majority of all the outstanding stock. However, it was pointed out that it would not have been necessary to buy these shares at par. The stocks of twenty-five of the leading railway systems were then selling at only a little more than half their par value. If the employees could continue to buy shares at this rate, it would be possible, by investing their savings and dividends, to secure a majority interest in these railway systems in three years. On the other hand, it was pointed out that extensive buying by a new group of investors would probably raise the price of shares, and it would not be possible for a very long period to continue buying them at half their par value. Unless this sent the price of the shares to a level considerably above par, it would still be possible to buy a controlling interest in five years.

The writer of the article further suggests that if the coöperative organization among railway employees for the purchase of American railways did not want to proceed by this wholesale method of investing in the stock of all the railways simultaneously, it could acquire first one railroad, and then another. "For example, the total outstanding stock of the New York Central Railroad is $250,000,000. The total outstanding stock of the Atchison, Topeka and Sante Fe Railroad is $346,000,000. The stocks of both companies are now selling below par (1920), but even if par had to be paid for them the railway employees of the United States could buy the stocks of both companies with that increase in their wages within a single year, and have a comfortable margin left to invest in the securities of other companies. The combined outstanding stock of the New York Central and the Pennsylvania in the East, and the Atchison, Topeka and Santa Fe and the Union Pacific in the West, amounts to $1,417,000,000. If the employees desired to acquire control first of the ownership and management of only these four great properties, they could buy a majority of the stocks of all of them at par with their recent increase in wages in fourteen months."

This prediction, made in 1920, has come near having a literal fulfilment, for in February, 1925, it was announced that 41,570 employees of the New York Central lines in twelve States and two Canadian provinces have become stockholders in the New York Central Railroad Company as a result of a special offering of the company's stock. Subscriptions were received for 96,900 shares, having a par value of $9,690,000. The offering of 35,000 shares was oversubscribed 176 per cent. In view of this heavy oversubscription, the company increased the amount of stock available for allotment to

68,747 shares. Prior to this offering the New York Central had 36,500 stockholders; there are now (February, 1925) 78,000 stockholders, more than twice the former number. One-fourth of all the employees in service have subscribed.

Another illustration is found in the fact that, early in 1925, 4,889 employees of the New York, New Haven and Hartford Railway subscribed for $857,000 worth of its bonds. These employee subscriptions ranged in amount from $100 up, the average being a little over $175. As a further move toward resident and away from absentee ownership, southern New England business men, who are the principal customers of the road, subscribed more than 53 per cent. of the total of the $23,000,000 of the loan.

If it is argued that laborers are not yet, in spite of their present prosperity, financially able to own the shops, factories, railroads, etc., with which they work, there is a perfectly conclusive answer. One prolonged strike will cost the laborers, directly and indirectly, more than it would cost them to buy a controlling interest in several of the leading establishments in their industry. By purchasing this controlling interest the laborers could at least give a demonstration of the way in which they think a business ought to be run and the wages it ought to pay. If the laborers can bear the cost of the strike, they can bear the equal cost of purchasing a controlling interest of this kind.

While this shows an interesting possibility, it would probably not be wise for laboring people with small sums per individual to risk their money in such investments as the common stock of railroads. This has been regarded in recent years as a somewhat hazardous form of investment. People with small sums to invest should never be advised to risk them on uncertain investments. However, it might be urged, on the other hand, that the hazardous nature of railway investments is due to the depredations of politicians and other predatory interests. Widespread ownership of railway securities, especially by laboring people, will be a very effective way of trimming the claws and filing the teeth of the cheap politicians, and will thus remove the chief factor in making railway securities dangerous investments.

It has long been the dream of social reformers that laborers should own the shops and factories in which they work. There are reasons for doubting that this would be as desirable from the standpoint of the workers as some have imagined. It is true that the workers would get the profits, if there were any, but it is equally true that they would also bear the losses if there were any. On the whole, losses are almost, if not quite, as common as profits.

Granting, however, that it would be desirable for the workers to own the establishments in which they work, there are three ways — two dishonest or revolutionary, and one honest — by which they may acquire them. The first and most direct of the dishonest methods is to seize them by force. This is the method openly advocated by the so-called "direct-actionists" and practiced by the Bolsheviki. Aside from the dishonesty of it, this method has serious drawbacks. The government must first be overthrown. Even then, the situation is not secure. Though this plan may put the present property in the hands of the worker, it cannot renew the property when it is worn out. There will be no new property to seize. People who never had enough thrift and forethought to buy and pay for property in the first place seldom have enough to keep the property up after they have gained it in some other way. When it runs down, there will be nothing to steal with which to keep up repairs. This the Bolsheviki have already discovered to their discomfiture.

Another dishonest way is to gain possession of the government and use its power to dispossess the present owners. This is frankly advocated by some of the Guild Socialists. It is to be done under the form of constitutional government, instead of in defiance of government. In the end, it will make little difference whether the force that is used to take property from one set of owners and give it to another is wielded by persons outside the government or by a perversion of governmental power.

If laborers want to own the shops in which they

work, there is an honest way. It is the way by which they may own the houses in which they live, their clothes, their household furniture, or anything else that they have not themselves made. That is, to buy and pay for them as other people do. This is the method by which manual workers have always become the owners of their tools. The joint-stock method of ownership is merely an adaptation to modern conditions. Even if they could take possession of the shops by force, they could only get repairs and replace worn-out plants by the method of purchase. There is no sound reason why they should gain possession of existing shops in any other way.

One of the strangest examples of the perverseness of the human mind is the tendency to misstate, or to accept without challenge the misstatement of others, regarding the relation of the worker to his tools. One of these misstatements is that the industrial revolution of the eighteenth century deprived manual laborers of the ownership of their tools. Of course it is impossible to deprive a person of ownership of something which he never owned. The new tools that came into existence with steam-driven machinery never were owned by manual workers. For the first time in history they are now in process of becoming in this country largely the property of those who work with them. In this connection it is fair to ask, "How did the manual workers of an earlier day become the owners of their tools?" The answer is that they either made them themselves or they bought them, usually the latter. The present tendency toward the purchase of shares in industrial plants is an application of the same method to modern conditions.

Another misstatement is that through government ownership, the workers would become, in effect, the owners of the plants in which they work. The employees in the city hall do not own the city hall, nor do they feel that they are working for themselves; the public school teachers do not own the school buildings, nor do they feel any more interest in their work than the teachers in private schools. The employees of the Federal Government do not own the buildings or the navy yards in which they work. Moreover, the employees themselves, in these publicly owned plants, do not feel that they are working for themselves or show any more interest in their work than do the employees in plants owned by private capitalists.

A third misstatement is to the effect that property in tools, machines, and industrial plants differs fundamentally from property in dwelling houses, furniture, clothing, cooking utensils, and other things commonly classed as consumers' goods. If it is found desirable that any class should own its own dwelling houses, household furniture, or clothes, the method of purchase is open. If it is found desirable that another class should own the land, livestock, and farming implements with which it works, the method of purchase is alike open. If it is found desirable that still another class should own the factories, shops, tracks or rolling stock with which it works, the method of purchase is open in this case also. When these various people buy the property in which or with which they work, they acquire a genuine ownership, and they will at once realize a significant difference between this and government ownership.

Another misstatement is to the effect that modern industrial plants are too big to be owned by their own workers. The joint-stock form of business organization was not designed primarily for the benefit of manual workers, but it would not have been much different from what it now is if it had been so designed. Neither state socialism, guild socialism, sovietism, nor the ordinary coöperative society presents a plan of organization so well suited to the needs of workers who desire to own their own plants as does the joint-stock corporation.

II

It was suggested earlier in this chapter that the laborer, like every one else who has small sums to invest, should be advised to invest with a view to safety rather than with a view to owning a controlling interest in the plants in which he works. In fact there is something to be said in favor of investing in some other plant than the one in which he works. If the plant should close down and the company become bankrupt at the same time, he would lose both his job and his investment, if he had invested his money in it; whereas there would be less likelihood of losing both at the same time if he had invested in another plant. However, he should not invest in any plant, either the one in which he works or any other, unless it is so old and well established as to reduce the probability of bankruptcy to the minimum. First, a savings deposit; second, insurance; third, the safest investment he can find; fourth, if he has anything more to invest, he may try new and promising investments. Of course, some one must invest in the securities of new and untried companies, otherwise no new and untried companies could ever be financed. But such investments are for men who have large sums to invest and who can give their whole time to the problem of investments, and can therefore acquire some expertness in this field.

It is noticeable that the companies that have been most successful with the policy of employee ownership are precisely those that have achieved the greatest stability, and whose securities are among the safest on the market. Their securities as a rule make good investments for laborers whether their own employees invest in them or not. A number of companies have had unsatisfactory experience with the plan of employee ownership precisely because their securities were not proper investments for people with small means. In a number of cases that have been reported, after laborers were persuaded to buy stock, the stock has declined in price. Then the company has felt bound to repurchase the stock, or been forced to do so in order to allay hostility.

This suggests a kind of economic dualism, much more scientific and satisfactory than any that has yet been suggested. Instead of advocating that large undertakings be taken over by the government and small ones left to private enterprise,[1] it would be better to advocate employee ownership of those undertakings that are so stabilized as to make success practically certain, depending only on sound and honest management, leaving to the speculative investor and promoter the experimental work of building up new enterprises. As soon as any of these become thoroughly stabilized, laborers could then be encouraged to buy them, thus releasing the speculative capital for still newer enterprises. In this way, the old and well-established industries would be owned by the workers, which is very much better than government ownership and politician operation, and ought to satisfy those who think that workers should own the tools with which they work.

An interesting bit of practical experience with the joint-stock form of organization was furnished many

[1] *See* an article by Edward A. Ross, entitled "The Case for Industrial Dualism", in the *Quarterly Journal of Economics* for May, 1924.

years ago by the Oneida Community. This community was formerly a communistic society of the most idealistic sort, having been founded by a religious group who were known as perfectionists, and who believed that for them the Kingdom of God had already arrived. It continued as a communistic society for about thirty years and then changed over to a New York State joint-stock corporation with a capital of $600,000, on a plan agreed to by all the members, whereby the shares in the new corporation were divided among men and women equally and according to years of membership in the community.[1] Even at that time the business had grown so much that the community was hiring some laborers that were not members of the communistic society. The business of the community has since grown to such magnitude that only a fraction of the work is now done by actual members. However, they have been selling common stock to employees for a number of years. In 1913 the stockholders set aside for distribution eight hundred shares, par value twenty-five dollars a share. Each year since then stockholders have made similar motions, the number of shares varying according to circumstances. In the year 1924 the amount voted was eight thousand shares. Practically all of them were subscribed for by July 1. All common stock is sold outright with-

[1] From a letter to the writer by S. R. Leonard, Vice-President of the Oneida Community, Limited.

out any strings of any kind. The par value is twenty-five dollars a share.

Here was a communistic society that was actually succeeding. Its business was growing and prospering. Yet its members decided that the joint-stock form of organization fitted their plans better, and apparently fulfilled their ideals satisfactorily. It is mentioned as an illustration of the writer's belief that this form of ownership supplies the American laborer with all he needs if he seriously desires to share in the ownership of the plant in which he works.

If we think of these vast sums accumulating, year after year, in the hands of laborers, we shall begin to see that the financial power of the American laboring people is a power to be reckoned with. All good citizens who are interested in the expansion of American industries should take account of this. Here is a new source of capital that may be so directed as to increase the productive power of the country and to create an additional demand for labor. Every time the laboring people of this country materially increase their savings and sound investments, they are helping themselves in two distinct ways. In the first place, they are gaining a new source of income. Even one hundred dollars that brings four per cent adds four dollars a year to the saver's income. In addition to this, and perhaps more important, is its effect upon the labor market. The more capital there is seeking investment, the more easily can new and productive enterprises be financed. The more new productive enterprises are properly financed and put in operation, the more jobs there are calling for men, the higher the wages of labor will be, or the less unemployment there will be. Laborers are beginning to appreciate this and to engage in what may be called the higher strategy of labor.

Closely related to employee ownership is customer ownership, since both represent forms of diffused ownership. A recent, striking example of this is in Philadelphia. In a six-day campaign beginning February 23, 1925, the Philadelphia Rapid Transit Company sold over 60,000 shares of 7 per cent. Cumulative Preferred Stock to 14,000 car riders. Stock could be purchased outright or it could be purchased on the weekly payment plan. Any street car conductor or subway-elevated cashier could act as collector. This plan of utilizing ordinary employees as stock-salesmen has come into use quite recently by various public service corporations.

On this subject, some sound reasoning and some pertinent facts are presented in a recent address by A. K. Baylor of the General Electric Company, before the National Electric Light Association at Birmingham, Alabama. He says in part:

As a matter of practical politics under our institutions it is only a question of whether the thrifty or the thriftless are in a voting majority. The solution of the problem of safeguarding personal property therefore appears to be to make the majority of our people capitalists. This will turn the tide and our political structure will become increasingly stable. The individual who has property investments yielding interest and dividends is a better citizen and particularly a better elector.

As a nation our outstanding contribution in human affairs has been material progress through industrial development and the dissemination of wages on a huge scale. All our actual currency goes through the hands of wage and salary earners several times a year. Never in the world's history, anywhere, has there been such a continuous and voluminous circulation of wealth. If all wage and salary earners would save but a fraction of what passes through their hands, investing and compounding it, they would accumulate in a single generation a sum approximating the present total wealth of the country which has been accumulating since the settlement of the Colonies. Why then cry out against those who have something through their own thrift or that of their ancestors? Rather should the envious critics make a beginning at emulating their example. The basis of the communistic anti-capitalistic creed being the primitive, predatory instinct, they would seize through the power of numbers, the moderates by political confiscation, the extremists by violence, but in either case without labor — what labor and thrift have acquired. The end is the same — to gain possessions. The individual communist, when provided with legitimate means of gaining and holding possessions, joins in the thrift class and the advocates of destruction find a diminishing following.

If we teach the lessons of thrift and make available safe investments in small denominations, it is not impossible to make capitalists of our majority in a comparatively short time — perhaps in one generation.

Within the last few years the plan of so-called "customer ownership" has been introduced by the electrical utility companies, their securities being sold to customers on the lines and on installments if desired. This plan has been applied, not only by the electric light and power companies but also by the telephone and other public services.

The movement took systematic form in 1914. Beginning with about $9,000,000, taken by individual customers in that year and sagging during the war, the customer investment rose to $16,000,000 in 1919 — $40,000,000 in 1920 — $80,000,000 in 1921 — $175,000,000 in 1922 and over $250,000,000 in 1923. This 1923 figure was one third of the total investment for the year in extensions of electric central station service. When this plan was adopted the question of financing extension was the principal consideration, as the cost of such financing through the usual banking channels at that time was excessive. Now electrical utility securities are as a class the most popular in the financial markets but the economic advantages of customer ownership and the response to this method of distribution have been so thoroughly demonstrated that it is being continued and must be extended even beyond available preferred stock issues if necessary to meet the demand. Such distribution is leading to direct public ownership — real ownership by the public — each in his own right, as against collective political ownership with its attendant wastefulness and inefficiency.

The insurance companies and in many cases the banks have large interests in the railroads and other utilities. It is estimated that there are 50,000,000 direct or indirect insurance policyholders and beneficiaries. It must be driven home to the public that when they support municipal or other political ownership or join in any movement inimical to these utility enterprises they are actually assisting an attempt to destroy the security of their own hard-earned savings, deposited in the banks, or invested in insurance.

The customer ownership fashion is spreading and is being followed in other industries. We are on the way to becoming a nation of capitalists and the electrical industry is the most outstanding factor in the movement.

CHAPTER SIX

"Ancestral Voices Prophesying War"

WAR may or may not have been the natural condition of mankind according as we define the word "natural." There is no doubt that men have always been compelled to struggle against enemies, either nonhuman or human. In the earlier stages the nonhuman enemies that were recognized and fought against were huge and ferocious beasts. In later stages they are mainly of the invisible sort, such as disease germs. The qualities of mind and temper which were required to fight vigorously and successfully against the huge and visible nonhuman enemies that threatened the lives of primitive men did not differ materially from those which were required for a vigorous and successful fight against human enemies. An enemy was something that had to be killed, the killing required a violent exercise of the fighting muscles, and these had to be driven by a fighting temper. Those who lacked the fighting temper had a poor chance of survival as compared with those who possessed it. This introduced a selective factor which tended to breed up a race with a fighting temper. The fighting temper had survival value. Those who possessed it were more likely to reproduce their kind than were those who lacked it. We who are now alive are the progeny of those who possessed it.

Like other inherited qualities, the fighting temper, though useful in its place, is in constant danger of perversion. It sometimes drives us to fight when there is no wisdom in fighting. Whenever we become irritated toward anything we naturally want to fight it. The child beats or breaks the mechanical toy that will not work; the man kicks the chair against which he has stumbled. He has been known to break his golf stick because of no fault of its own. It sometimes requires severe self-discipline for a teamster to refrain from swearing at or beating his mules, even though wisdom would counsel gentleness. These and other expressions of the fighting temper are perfectly "natural", but what is natural in this sense is not always identical with what is wise. They are wise forms of behavior so long as they are directed toward real enemies of the kind that threaten life. They are unwise when directed toward those irritating friends that are, on the whole, useful to ourselves but sometimes stubborn and intractable.

Much of the fighting program, in what Mr. Warren Stone has called the second or fighting stage of the labor movement, was the mere expression of this primitive desire to fight whatever irritates or vexes us. When directed against an enemy whom we want exterminated or thinned out, it is wise enough. The fighting temper was developed in us for the purpose of thinning out or exterminating whatever threatened our lives. It was not given us for the purpose of thinning out or exterminating things that are useful to us, though it is sometimes perverted to such a use.

When the fighting temper was directed against employers it was calculated to decrease some of the things that labor needed to have increased. Strategically, this part of labor's program was about as wise as it would be for producers to try to reduce the number of consumers, or for consumers to try to reduce the number of producers; for cranberry growers to try to discourage the production of sugar, or for sugar producers to try to discourage the production of cranberries; for farmers who need capital to try to drive away those who have capital, or for capitalists to try to drive away those who need it.

This perversion of the fighting instinct extends far beyond our treatment of those inanimate things and dumb animals that vex us. It extends over the whole field of human relations and produces most of the evil that is found there. Many a quarrel — one might almost say, most quarrels — originate here, though sometimes, no matter how the quarrel started, there is not much that the one who is on the defensive can do except to defend himself. But for this tendency to fight whatever angers us, not many modern wars would ever have begun. Some one cannot get what he wants by diplomacy and persuasion; perhaps he finds the other party a little unreasonable and hard to persuade. It is very natural, but unwise, to yield to the impulse to fight him. So far as the aggressor is concerned, Norman Angell, the most bellicose living apostle of pacificism, in his "Great Illusion" is sound in his reasoning. To that extent war is merely this perverted fighting instinct applied to cases where wisdom counsels gentleness. Two fundamental objections may be raised to the rest of his reasoning. First, he did not answer the question: What can the attacked party do but defend itself? Perhaps it would be better to say that his answer is one that insults the intelligence of every reader. Second, he did not seem to see that the same reasoning applied to labor troubles as to international disputes. That primitive behaviorism which expresses itself in the desire to fight whatever vexes us is as evident in a labor dispute as in an international dispute. The reasons against fighting are even stronger in the field of industrial relations than they are in the field of international relations.

An enemy nation comes more nearly resembling one of those ancient and hereditary enemies that were the external and threatening cause of our having developed a fighting temper, than any enemy that we are likely to find in industrial relations. There might be some economic advantage in conquering another people and taking their land. We took land away from the American Indians. It is hard to justify on moral grounds, but there is no doubt that we gained by it. A similar thing might happen elsewhere. Of course, if the Indians had been ready to develop the resources of this continent and then trade with Europeans, both might have gained by that process. If that were true, it would have been to our interest to develop friendly trade with the Indians rather than to rob them of their land. However much we may argue over this point, there is not the slightest doubt that, in industrial relations, it pays better to cherish and nurture your "enemy", or, rather, your irritating friend and supporter, than to exterminate him.

Let us suppose that the growers of strawberries become incensed against the consumers because they will not buy strawberries at a price high enough to pay the cost of production. Unless the fighting temper is restrained, the growers will do diametrically the wrong thing. They will start a fight against consumers. To fight consumers is to discourage them, drive them away, or even exterminate them. Here is a new kind of "enemy" that producers need to have multiplied instead of thinned out. Their ancestral psychology in the form of a fighting temper fitted them to deal with the old kind of an enemy that needed to be thinned out or exterminated. It unfits us all to deal with this new kind of enemy that we need to have increased. Nothing but calculated self-interest, *i. e.*, economic intelligence, can teach us how to deal with this new kind of enemy.

Most of our "enemies" in the present economic situation are of this kind. Of course, one may contend that they are not really enemies. It takes a process of reasoning, however, to arrive at that conclusion. Our economic behaviorism never taught us that. Anything that irritates us arouses our fighting temper. We hate it. "Hates any man the thing he would not kill?" In the preceding illustration, the producer's attitude toward the consumer will be determined by the question whether his calculated self-interest gets the better of his fighting temper or *vice versa*. If his calculated self-interest prevails, he will try to multiply the number of consumers. If his fighting temper gains the mastery, he will act as though he wanted to thin them out, or at least he will act in a manner that is calculated to drive consumers away rather than to attract them.

When you are driven by your fighting temper, you are willing to suffer injury yourself if only you can inflict a greater injury upon the one with whom you are dealing. When you are guided by your calculated self-interest, you are perfectly willing that the one with whom you are dealing should gain some benefit if only you can gain a benefit yourself. They who are appealing to the fighting temper of laboring people and are trying to stir up their resentment are really not so anxious to benefit the laborers as they are to inflict an injury on the capitalist or the employer. No one in his right mind ever dreamed that the "ca' canny"[1] policy could be of any possible benefit to laborers. It could only do harm to capitalist employers. Sabotage or any method of doing injury to the property of employers, if generally indulged in, cannot fail to discourage business enterprise by increasing the risk and cost of doing business. If it should become the general practice of labor organizations, every business man would have to anticipate some loss from this source, and it would undoubtedly deter some of them from entering upon new business enterprises, especially where there was some doubt as to whether such enterprises would pay or not. This additional cost might easily turn the balance from profit to loss. Even in the case of an enterprise already in operation, it might make the difference between bankruptcy and solvency.

Where men are deterred from investing in business enterprises because of any unusual risk or cost, there must necessarily be less business expansion than there would be if that special risk or cost did not exist. Where business does not expand, there are not so many jobs for laboring men as there would be if business did expand. No laborer or group of laborers who followed their calculated self-interest would do anything to hinder business expansion.

[1] This consists in being exceedingly parsimonious of one's labor, in doing as little as possible in order to make every job last as long as possible.

They would rather do anything they could, short of accepting lower wages or worse conditions, to encourage business expansion, knowing that if business expands for other reasons, it tends to create higher wages or better conditions. But when laborers are driven by their fighting temper, they are willing to accept lower wages and worse conditions if only they can inflict greater losses on their employers, whom they are led by their anger to regard as their enemies. This does not mean, of course, that laborers welcome these injuries to themselves any more than other fighters welcome wounds. Fighters merely embark upon an attempt to do injury to some one else, knowing that they must expect to receive wounds themselves. The certainty of receiving wounds does not deter the fighter if he thinks that he can inflict greater wounds than he receives. It is in this sense that those leaders who urge the "ca' canny" policy, or persuade laborers to engage in sabotage or other destructive measures, show their willingness that the laborers should suffer injury in order that greater injury might be inflicted on capitalist employers.

While the "ca' canny" policy is the meanest and the silliest of all expressions of the fighting temper, it is not necessarily the most destructive. Everything that is done by "labor" or in the name of "labor", that is calculated to add to the risk and the cost of doing business, tends to discourage young men from going into business and older men from expanding their business enterprises, and hastens the bankruptcy of still others. If we choose an illustration entirely dissociated from labor troubles, this will be perfectly clear because our feelings will not obscure our judgment or defeat our attempt to understand the problem. Among the risks of business is that of fire. Suppose that something should happen to increase the risk of fire. Does any one doubt that this would be an additional cost? If the factory owner buys insurance it will cost him more than it did when the risk was less. If he carries his own insurance he must make a larger allowance if he would avoid bankruptcy. In either case, if he is a marginal manufacturer who is making little or no profit, he must have enough larger margin between expenses and receipts to enable him to carry this new insurance. That is, he must get his labor and his raw materials a little cheaper, he must sell his product a little higher, or he must, sooner or later, go out of business. If he gets his labor cheaper or sells his product at a higher price, laborers will be paying a part of the cost. If the factory closes, a certain number of laborers will lose their jobs and will have to seek jobs somewhere else.

A new item of cost of this kind would probably not cause the bankruptcy of any except the weaker establishments, that is, those that are making little or no profits. The stronger ones would be able to readjust themselves. But even if only the weaker ones go into bankruptcy because of their inability to get labor and supplies enough cheaper or to sell their products enough higher to cover the new item of cost, still some laborers would be thrown out of work. There will, in that case, be fewer jobs because there will be fewer business houses running.

If these results follow from a new item of risk or cost, such as fire, which the laborers have no part in creating, is it likely that the same results could be escaped if the new item was created by the laborers themselves? Sabotage might conceivably take the form of incendiarism; if so, it would increase the risk of fire and raise the rates of insurance. The results would be as bad for labor as though the increased fire risk was described as an "act of God."

Let us apply this principle to labor troubles in general. Let the reader imagine himself in the position of a young man looking forward to a career, with a very slight leaning toward some manufacturing business. Before deciding to go into business for himself instead of continuing in a salaried position, he would, of course, consider very carefully the ins and outs of an independent business career as well as those of a salaried position. Of course, if he has very strong leanings one way or the other, slight considerations would not affect him. There are always, in any group of young men about to decide on a career, a certain number who have no very noticeable leanings in either direction and who are having a good deal of difficulty in deciding which way to turn. Such young men are influenced one way or the other by circumstances that would not affect those whose minds have been definitely made up on the basis of strong preferences. Let the reader put himself in the position of one of these young men who have difficulty in deciding.

If, when considering the ins and outs of a business career, you decide that there is no great likelihood of labor troubles of any kind, one possible difficulty is eliminated. You are much more likely to choose a business career under these conditions than you are if you know that you will have to face labor troubles of any sort. If you are a hard, belligerent person who loves a fight because you are possessed of a strong fighting temper, this may make little difference; but if you are somewhat sensitive and do not like to be misunderstood and called hard names by your own workers, but desire to be well thought of by all men, particularly by those who are associated with you in your business, you will shrink from a business career when you foresee that it means taking arms against a sea of labor troubles. Those who deliberately choose business careers under such circumstances will be the hard-fisted fighters, unless there is a chance for unusual profit in the business. This might very well happen. That is to say, if an abnormal number should choose wage and salaried positions and an abnormally small number should choose independent business careers, the few who do choose business careers will be able to hire men for low wages and at low salaries; there being many applicants for jobs and few employers, this result would follow as a matter of course. There would also be comparatively few manufacturing establishments running and a small supply of manufactured products. This would make the products sell at a high price. Low wages and salaries on the one hand, and high prices on the other, are the normal result of any tendency that discourages men from entering upon manufacturing careers as independent business men.

If we take an extreme case, such as wholesale brigandage, which is still found in some backward countries, we can see this principle in actual operation. No one is encouraged to start any productive enterprise. There are few jobs for laborers, and consequently wages are low and unemployment almost universal. On the other hand, prices have to be high enough to leave a wide margin between labor cost and price to enable those venturesome manufacturers who go into the manufacturing business to cover their losses. Less extreme cases, such as ordinary sabotage, do not produce such acute results, but the tendency is in the same general direction.

If sensitive souls like yourself are uniformly discouraged from trying independent business careers because you anticipate labor troubles of various kinds, there will be fewer business men of your sort. There will be more men seeking salaried positions and wage positions, with fewer business men to employ them, than there would be if conditions were safer. If conditions can be made so safe that every capable person, however sensitive he may be, would be encouraged to go into business for himself if he saw a fair opportunity to sell a product for enough to pay the cost, there would generally be small margins between labor costs and prices; in fact, laborers would get a large share of the joint products of labor, capital, and enterprise.

If you are not very well informed, you might flatter yourself into thinking that while other men might have labor troubles, you would escape; that is, you might imagine that you would treat your laborers so well that you would never have any difficulty. In this you would be mistaken. To begin with, you would not be immune against a sympathetic strike. In the second place, you might have to use coal in your business. If so, you would need to keep a larger coal pile ahead in order to insure you against the stoppage of your works if there should be a coal strike or a railroad strike, either of which would make it impossible for you to get coal for current use. If you did not keep a large coal pile ahead, your business would promptly close down in such a case as this. If you do keep a large coal pile, your overhead expenses are increased thereby. Somebody must pay this overhead. Your profits may be so large as to enable you to pay it without shifting it back onto your own laborers or forward onto the buyers of your product. If, however, you are not one of those fortunate manufacturers who make large profits but are somewhere near the margin where profits are small or nonexistent, you cannot possibly carry this extra charge. You may shift it one way or the other, or go out of business. That is, if you stay in business, you must succeed in getting a little higher price for your product or in getting labor and supplies a little cheaper in order to enable you to carry this extra overhead.

Your extra overhead cost will not be confined to your coal pile. Every form of raw material needed in your business must be kept on hand in larger quantities than would be necessary if there were never any danger of a strike in some other industry cutting off your supply. In addition to this, your salary list must be enlarged if you are to avoid misunderstanding and trouble with your own laborers. You must hire personnel managers and a numberof others whose business is solely to keep your laborers in a friendly attitude. These are made necessary by the fact that there are always agitators trying to create misunderstanding and hostility among your laborers toward yourself. This extra cost, like other extra costs, must be paid by somebody, either by yourself, by the laborers you hire in the form of lower wages, or by the buyers of your product in the form of higher prices.

The fact that every man who goes into business for himself has to figure on all these extra items of expense will deter a sufficient number to enable the bolder ones to get higher prices for their products or to get their labor at lower wages. If these artificial items of cost could be eliminated more factories would be started, which would necessitate either the paying of higher wages in order to get laborers, or offering goods at lower prices in order to sell the increasing quantity. This would reduce the incomes of independent business men at least as low as they are under more dangerous conditions; but there would be more of them in business, and they would be able to pay these slightly higher wages or to sell at slightly lower prices because of the lower cost of doing business.

All those labor policies which are dictated by the fighting temper rather than by calculated self-interest tend, in the long run, to undo or nullify many of the advantages that labor organizations gain through more constructive methods. The strike itself, even when unaccompanied by violence, sabotage, or any other method of terrorism, adds appreciably to the cost of doing business in those industries that incur the risk of failure through their inability to get raw materials and other necessary things.

When does a strike cease to be a means of defence

and begin to be a means of extortion? This is a question of growing importance in this country, and it is certain to become acute before very long. When laborers who are already more prosperous than the average consumer of their products resort to the strike in order to gain still further advantage, the buyers of the product will begin to perceive that the strike is becoming a means of extortion. So long as the strike was used by laborers who were in a condition of poverty, it might be condemned on purely abstract grounds, but a good-natured and tolerant people would not condemn it very severely in practice. If the present tendencies in the economic development of the United States continue, it will not be long before laborers of every class are lifted out of a condition of poverty into a condition of prosperity. If they continue to use the strike, it will impose a severe test upon the patience and good nature of the American people. The striking laborers can then no longer appeal to sympathy.

There are some items in present labor programs which may seem to be constructive in their nature, even though they are not. The appearance of constructiveness is sometimes due to poor economic teaching. There are a great many people, both within and without the labor unions, who believe that a reduction of output in some way tends to increase wages or the demand for labor. That is to say, if each laborer only does half as much, it looks to some people as though it would take twice as many laborers to do the work. If we insist on having as much as we did before and are able to pay for it, will this not increase the demand for laborers to do the necessary work?

The fallacy of this argument is easily shown the moment you try to extend it outside of a single field of production. Let us grant, for the sake of argument, that if all cotton-mill operatives should reduce their output by one half, it would take twice as many operatives to spin and weave all the cotton that is now grown. However, if the cotton growers likewise cut down their output by one half, difficulties would begin to arise. If, as the result of their reduction of output, there is only one half as much cotton to be spun and woven, there would be no more employment for labor in cotton manufacturing than there was before the fashion of reducing output was started. The only real result would be that the world would have to get along with half as many cotton goods as it might otherwise have. If we again extend the policy of reducing output to other industries that produce the things that cotton-mill operatives want, the difficulties increase. If shoemakers, tanners, and all others who have anything to do with the making of shoes, reduce their output by one half, there will be only one half as many shoes to exchange for the small supply of cotton cloth, and the ratio of pairs of shoes to cotton cloth will be about what it would have been if everybody had continued to produce at full capacity. So, if we go on and extend this policy to every industry, the net result will be that only half as many goods will be produced, and the relative shares of each class of producers will remain about the same as it is now. In short, it will make everybody about twice as poor as he is now, and nobody will gain anything by it.

A very good test of the soundness of any economic policy is to imagine that it is extended until it becomes universal. A universal cutting down of output would obviously reduce the sum total of the world's wealth, and compel us all to get along with fewer of the things we now want.

It is sometimes argued that there is no essential difference between reducing the product of each laborer and reducing the number of laborers. The analogy would be correct if, instead of merely reducing the number of laborers, we reduce everything that enters into production. If we cut the land in half, the capital in half, and labor of every kind and condition in half, the effect upon the relative shares will be very much the same as though the quantities of these things remained the same, but each one did only half as much work. But if we reduce the number of manual laborers to one half the present number, and leave everything else as abundant as it now is, we have a very different situation. For each manual worker there will be a larger quantity of supplementary agents of production, — more and better tools, more and better land, more and better direction, more skilled technicians and other people to help make manual labor more effective. Merely to slow down production does not change the ratio between manual labor and these other factors.

If a decrease in the number of laborers by the restriction of immigration tends to increase wages, why does not a decrease in the amount of work done by each laborer have the same tendency? There are two reasons why it does not. In the first place, a decrease in the amount of work done by each laborer tends to decrease the product of industry without decreasing the number of men among whom the product is to be divided. This would leave less for each man. On the other hand, even though a decrease in the number of laborers should decrease the product of industry, it also decreases the number of men among whom the product is divided. There need therefore be no decrease in the amount going to each man; in fact, there is likely to be an increase.

In the second place, if each laborer slows down, shortens his hours, or in any other way does less work, the tools, machines and other equipment with which he works must also slow down, shorten their hours, or do less work. If the number of laborers is decreased, there is no necessary slowing down or shortening of the hours of the equipment with which they work. If the hours of labor are cut down from eight to six, unless it is then arranged to work double shifts, the whole equipment works but six hours. It will take as much capital in the form of buildings, engines, machines and tools, also as many foremen, superintendents, etc., to equip and direct a given number of men working six hours as an equal number working eight hours. If it takes more laborers to produce a given quantity of goods when they work six hours than when they work eight, it also takes a larger quantity of these capital goods. If shortening the hours of labor increases the demand for labor, it increases the demand for capital in equal degree. Since the demand for labor and for capital maintains the same ratio, there is no reason to suppose that labor's share of the product would increase more than capital's. In fact, the relative shares would remain about the same. If there should be a smaller product to divide, both labor and capital would lose.

If, however, as suggested above, reducing the number of hours to six should result in working double shifts, so that each piece of capital worked twelve hours while each laborer worked six, it would then take less capital to equip a given number of laborers. The demand for capital would not increase to correspond with the demand for labor, and labor would eventually get a larger share. This, however, could not possibly follow from a mere slowing down of labor, or from any plan of reducing output except the one mentioned, namely, combining shorter hours with a double shift.

Aside from the question of changing the relative shares in distribution, it is sometimes suggested that with our improved technique of production, we could continue to have all that we need, even though industry in general slowed down or reduced its hours of work. That is to say, if not only the labor, but the machinery and the management in every industry worked but four hours a day, it may be admitted that no class would gain at the expense of any other class; yet it may be maintained that we could still produce as much as we really need.

Not only is the four-hour day a future possibility; it is a possibility now. That is, we could produce all that is actually necessary for a healthy existence if we would really work four hours a day. Unless, however, it can be shown that we can now produce as much in four hours as in eight, the conclusion follows that we would have to do without a good many things that we now enjoy. Possibly we might be better off with less, but would we like it as well?

When it is said that technical improvements will soon enable us to get along with four hours' work a day, it can only mean that some day, owing to the improvements that are soon to come, we shall be able to produce as much in four hours as we now produce in eight or ten and that we can then have as many and as expensive things for four hours' work as we now get for eight or ten. It is equally true that with our present improvements we could now produce in four hours as much as was produced a generation or so ago in ten or twelve, and that we could therefore live as well by working four hours as our grandfathers did by working ten or twelve. But who wants to live to-day as our grandfathers did? It is equally pertinent to ask, will our grandsons be content to live as we do, even though they could do so by working four hours a day? They may prefer to work eight hours and have twice as much as we now have rather than to work four hours and have as much as we have.

The question in its broadest aspect is simply this: do we prefer to take our increasing prosperity in the form of more goods or in the form of more leisure? Nations as well as individuals answer this question differently. Those nations where it is the general habit to take prosperity in the form of more leisure, do not seem to be attracting many immigrants, even from among the advocates of the four-hour day. Those that take their prosperity in the form of more goods are the only ones that seem to attract immigrants.

Without going into too much detail, it is safe to say that the presumption is always against any policy that is dictated by the fighting temper rather than by calculated self-interest. Any policy that is designed, first, to do injury to somebody else, is not likely to result in any positive good to the one who carries out that policy. When laboring people learn to think in terms of their self-interest rather than in terms of their fighting temper, they will lend cold and inattentive ears to the agitator who appeals to the baser passions of jealousy, covetousness and resentment, and also to the one who appeals merely to their fighting temper, — even though the fighting temper is useful in its place. The Great Illusion has been applied to the idea that anything was to be gained by international war. The Greater Illusion may properly be applied to the idea that in our economic relationships anything is to be gained by substituting destructive war for productive emulation, or that as much is to be gained for oneself or some one else by trying to do injury as by trying to render a service or confer a benefit. Aside from all questions of morals, there is economic wisdom in the proposition that no one is likely to gain anything in this world unless he contributes also to the gain of some one else.

The indulgence of their fighting temper has cost the laboring people of this country larger sums than one would care to name. The cost, both direct and indirect, of strikes alone has run into hundreds of millions. Boeckel records [1] that one strike of the typographical union cost that organization alone over fourteen million dollars. This is only the direct

[1] The *Forum*. Page 432. April, 1924.

cost of a minor strike. The indirect costs must have been much greater. If a fraction of these enormous costs had been put into the purchase of the shares of the more stable of our corporations, the laborers would already own a controlling interest in a good many of them. If they had done that, we should already have realized that dream of social reformers in which the workers should own the tools with which they work, even though the tools are of the modern sort that can only be owned by the joint-stock method. It is time for our laborers to stop indulging that expensive luxury — the fighting temper — and begin the more remunerative method of buying and paying for the control over industry that they so much desire.

CHAPTER SEVEN

The Higher Strategy of Labor

I

SIGNS are multiplying on every hand that American labor policy is entering upon a new stage. They who are still thinking in terms of the old labor policy naturally think that the labor movement in this country is receding. They who understand it better realize that it is making a most notable advance, and that it is already so far in advance of the labor movement in other countries as to nullify all comparisons. This new development is recognized by the more far-sighted leaders in the ranks of labor itself and also by the shrewder observers on the outside. One of the shrewdest of these, the astute editor of the *Villager*, has the following to say:

Labor is no longer the under dog, fighting with brute strength, growling, biting, and chewing.[1] That period is done. That chapter is closed. Sheer physical force has taken Labor as far now as physical force can take it. Threats and blows have obtained all there is to be obtained by that method; Labor has got all it can get by violence. There is a great

[1] *See* an editorial entitled "Labor and the Injunction", in the *Villager* for October 18, 1924.

deal more to be got, however, and it is to be got by head-work, not by fist-work.

In the first period, Labor's purpose was to make the community fear it. In this new period, Labor must get the community not to fear it — this is Labor's task now. Labor threatened the country with its power. Now it must impress the country with its wisdom. Labor got what it wanted by making us see it as a power which could destroy our order, destroy our production, destroy our prosperity. To get what it now wants, Labor must obliterate this notion, and put in the place of it the confidence that Labor is a preserver and a developer, a power which, given its way, will preserve our order, show us how to increase our production, make for our greater prosperity.

The change from primitive fighting tactics of labor to the higher strategy of labor involves a change in the type of leadership that comes to the top. The old type of labor leader was the fighter; he fought his way to the top by overcoming all opposition within the ranks of labor. Having fought his way to the top, he became the leader in the fight against capital.

Here we should notice a wide difference between the rank and file of laboring men and the leaders that the earlier labor movement produced. The rank and file of laboring men are good fellows, peaceable, industrious, willing to work and anxious to do an honest day's work for an honest day's pay. Wide personal acquaintance among laboring men will convince any one of this fact.

It may seem a little mysterious that men of this type should be led by men of almost the opposite type. However, this is not unusual in human affairs. A straightforward, honest business man — that is, honest up to his lights — will sometimes employ a pettifogging lawyer if for no other reason than that such a lawyer will get him what he wants. He will employ such a lawyer and profit by his fighting qualities, even though, in his heart, he despises such lawyers and all their works. Men who are reasonably honest and straightforward will sometimes support politicians of the most blatant sort, merely because they think such politicians will get them what they want in the way of protective legislation, labor legislation, or something else that is conceived to be good for one class or another. Yet even these men despise the blatherskite as heartily as the rest of us do. College professors, even, have been known to support men for university presidencies whose sole fitness for the job was the ability either to wheedle money out of rich men or to lobby before a legislature for appropriations. These college professors think as poorly of such presidents as any one else, but if they are not very scrupulous, they are quite willing to endure these disagreeable qualities for the sake of the pecuniary advantage that may come to themselves. When other people will employ lawyers or support politicians or college presidents to do things which they would not be willing to do themselves, we should not be surprised that laboring men should support leaders who would not scruple at methods in which the rank and file of laborers would not themselves take part. In short, neither laboring people nor any other group are to be judged wholly by the kind of leaders they support.

The country is full of self-appointed leaders of the people who remind themselves strongly of Lincoln and who stridently proclaim the resemblance. The more waspish they are, and the more they appeal to the baser qualities in human nature, the more they are impressed that they are the reincarnations of Lincoln. If they have been trained in the forms of religion and are not overmodest, as such people seldom are, they are very likely to remind themselves of Jesus.

There are two distinct types of leadership in the world. One type — and this is always the most numerous — strives for leadership by appealing to the worst that is in human nature, namely, the belligerent, rancorous and covetous feelings.[1] It goes before the people and tells them a great deal about their rights, their wrongs, and their grievances; but tells them nothing about their opportunities and

[1] *See* the author's "Principles of National Economy", Ginn and Company, 1921; especially Part viii, ch. 51. Also his "Essays in Social Justice", ch. 14, Harvard University Press, 1915.

their obligations. It stirs up envy and hatred rather than the spirit of mutual understanding and co-operation. The other and less numerous type tells the people a great deal about their opportunities and obligations and nothing about their rights, their wrongs and their grievances. The one exploits the wrongs and the grievances of those to whom they are talking, and denounces the sins of other people, who are not present to defend themselves or to state their case. The other talks to the people about their own duties and about what they owe to themselves, to society and to the world.

The results of one type of leadership are resentment, envy, and covetousness. The results of the other type of leadership are a deepening of the sense of duty and a wider knowledge of opportunities. The one kind is the work of demagogues, though they usually pose as heroes. The other is the work of men of courage and conviction, though they do not pose as such. It does not take any courage, for example, to talk to laboring men about the sins of capitalists, or to capitalists about the sins of laboring men. It takes a good deal of courage to talk to either class about its own sins and its obligations to other classes.

By way of illustration, let us look at the case of the Negroes of the South. They undoubtedly have their rights, their wrongs, and their grievances; and there are plenty of leaders to tell them about such things and to stir up the feeling of envy and resentment. They also have their opportunities and their obligations; and they had Booker T. Washington to talk about these things.

The writer suggests an experiment to any reader who is in doubt as to which of the two types of leadership was represented by Booker T. Washington, Abraham Lincoln, or any of the other really constructive leaders of the world, not excluding even the Founder of Christianity. Let him take a sheet of paper and rule it in two columns. Then let him make a careful study of the recorded utterances of Booker T. Washington. Let him put in the left-hand column every citation in which Booker T. Washington said anything to any Negro or group of Negroes that was calculated to stir up bad feeling. Let him put in this column everything that he told them about their grievances, their wrongs, or even their rights. In the right-hand column let him put every citation in which Booker T. Washington told the Negroes to whom he was speaking of something that they could do for themselves and of what they owed in the way of duty and obligation to society, to the nation, and to civilization. Then let him make a comparison of the two columns. On another sheet of paper, ruled in the same way, let him record the results of a similar study of all the published utterances of Abraham Lincoln. Let him put in the left-hand column every citation where Lincoln tried to stir up bad feeling or resentment. Let him put in this column also every citation where Lincoln told the people whom he was addressing anything about their rights, their wrongs, or their grievances, either real or imagined. In the other column let him include every citation where Lincoln tried to conciliate and bring about a better understanding, and where he told the people whom he was addressing something about their opportunities and their obligations. Having done this, let him compare the two columns. If the reader is interested in going further with this experiment, let him rule a third sheet of paper in the same way, and proceed to record the published utterances of the Founder of Christianity, putting again in the left-hand column every citation where He tried to create bitterness of feeling, or where He tried to stir up resentment, or where He told the people whom He was addressing anything about their rights, their wrongs, or their grievances. In the other column let him include every citation where He told the people of their opportunities and their obligations. He will see a great similarity among these three sheets of paper. He will find the left-hand columns either absolutely blank or almost blank, and the right-hand columns full.

Then let him try the same experiment with any three of the raucous leaders of popular discontent of the present day, and let him compare these three sheets with the other three. Of course the leaders who are the subject of the second study, and whose records are found on the second group of three sheets, pose as the leaders of discontent. They and their followers will resent this comparison. They will claim that the purpose of such a study as is here proposed is to allay discontent and to ally the readers and all moral agencies, including the churches, against the forces of discontent. This would not be an accurate statement, however, because there are two distinct kinds of discontent. It all depends on which kind of discontent one has in mind. The purpose of the leaders of the constructive sort is to create discontent of the right kind as truly as it is the purpose of the destructive group to create discontent of the wrong kind.

There is one kind of discontent that is based on egotism and supreme contentment with self. There is another kind of discontent that is based upon modesty, self-criticism, and discontent with self. If I am a supreme egotist and so thoroughly contented with myself as to be utterly unable to imagine that I can possibly be in the wrong, I am absolutely certain to be very much discontented with other people, with society, with the industrial system, and with the world in general, especially if I think I am not treated as well as I ought to be treated. The destructive kind of leadership flatters self-contented egotism and stirs up discontent with everything except self. It is very safe to be this kind of a leader.

On the other hand, if I am sufficiently modest, or sufficiently given to self-criticism to be able to see my own faults, and not to be infuriated when they are pointed out to me, I may become discontented with myself, with my own morals, my own education, my own industry, my own thrift, my own wisdom, my own constructive achievements. I then belong to the discontented class, but my discontent is the kind that begins at home — where other good things begin. I am then ready for progress and improvement. I can respond to the kind of constructive leadership that was achieved by Booker T. Washington, Abraham Lincoln, and other great leaders, not excluding Jesus himself. There is hope for me and for every one else who is in the same mood. A nation made up of such people will be a very progressive nation. This progress, when it comes, will be the result of discontent, but it will be discontent of the right kind. It is the only kind of discontent that ought ever to be called divine. The other kind is devilish.

Labor leaders may be grouped in the same classes as those other leaders whom we have described. The destructive leaders are those who appeal to the primitive fighting passions. The constructive leaders are those who show the way to larger opportunities; who realize that the surest and safest way to increase your own prosperity is to increase your own usefulness. The destructive leaders are still engaged in the immediate strategy of battle; the constructive leaders are thinking, acting, and speaking in terms of the higher strategy. The destructive leaders merely give expression to the primitive, fighting instinct which would destroy whatever irritates it or appears, in the moment of passion, to be an enemy; which encourages a man to break a chair against which he has stumbled, to throw clubs at his chickens if they do not come when they are called, or to engage in other perfectly natural but perfectly futile activities. The constructive leaders are those who think ahead and try to get their followers to act in accordance with far-sighted wisdom rather than in accordance with primitive passion.

In an article cited in a previous chapter by Warren S. Stone, in the *World's Work* for November, 1924, that writer says:

"Organized labor in the United States has gone through three cycles (some of the unions are still in the second). The first was the period during which class consciousness was being aroused. It was necessary at the outset to evolve a sense of solidarity, before there could be any collective effort toward better wages and better working conditions. The railway brotherhoods, by the very nature of their occupation, were the first to emerge from this period and to exhibit a remarkable cohesion. I think I may say that with but few exceptions every competent locomotive engineer in the United States, Canada, and Mexico is now a member of our organization. We have ninety-six per cent. of the total in this country.

The second stage was a defensive struggle for the principle of collective bargaining. This was and is a period of warfare. It involves the use of force, sometimes economic and sometimes physical, on both sides. There are labor leaders to-day who think only in terms of force. They cannot believe that the ends and aims of labor can possibly be achieved through understanding and coöperation. They deny that there is an actual identity of interest between the employer and the employed. Even when there is no open warfare under such leadership, even when there are no strikes, there is no real peace; there is only an armistice, a breathing spell before another fight. . . .

The third cycle or phase lies in constructive development toward a system of coöperation rather than war; and the most striking evidence of this phase is the labor bank."

II

At this point we should stop to notice the essential difference between primitive fighting tactics and the higher economic strategy. In primitive warfare you gain in proportion as you thin out your enemies. The more uncomfortable you can make it for them, the fewer there will be of them and the better it will be for you. All our ancestors for thousands of years had to think in these terms. It will take some time to breed this idea out of our people. The clear, cold fact is that in the modern economic world you gain in proportion as you increase the number of your enemies on the market. Take the simple case of producer and consumer. When they are dickering over prices they are opponents. If they become irritated at one another, they are likely to fall back into the old way of thinking and to treat each other as enemies. If the producers are dominated by this ancestral habit of thought, they will hate all consumers.

It is, of course, obvious to the most elementary student of economics that what producers should do if they knew their own interest would be to try to increase the number of consumers. What they are very likely to do when they become angry is to try to thin them out.[1]

This is the principle that runs through all our economic life. Goods are not produced by labor; they are produced by labor *and* capital. More accurately, goods are not produced by present labor alone, they are produced by present labor in combination with past labor that is stored up or embodied in the form of tools, machines, and other equipment. We call this form of stored-up labor by the name of capital. It is a necessary ingredient in any large industry. If one ingredient is missing, there is not much demand for the other.

[1] For a more detailed discussion of this point, *see* chapter six, *ante*.

Take for illustration a new farming community where the farmers have not yet equipped their farms with the necessary tools, buildings, live stock, etc. What they need is more capital. Of course it would be a fine thing if they had capital of their own. If they do not, the next best thing is to be able to borrow it. But if there is very little loanable capital to be had and very few lenders, the farmers will bid against one another for that small amount and force up the rate of interest. It would be very natural for the farmers to be incensed against the money lenders and to make war upon them, in accordance with their inherited psychology. This would discourage other money lenders from coming to such a community or sending their capital there. The farmers would clearly be doing themselves harm rather than good by behaving in this perfectly natural way. They must realize that what is natural is not always identical with what is wise or economic. If they behaved in accordance with economic wisdom, they would try to attract as many lenders and as much loanable capital as possible to that community. This would give them lower interest rates and a more abundant equipment for their farms. If they behaved in accordance with the primitive fighting tactics, they would tend to drive lenders of loanable capital out of the community. If they behaved in terms of higher strategy, they would offer such terms and inducements as would attract lenders of loanable capital.

In the case of labor and industries in general, the same principle follows. In proportion as capital is scarce relatively to the labor supply, in that proportion will capitalists be well off and laborers badly off. What the laborers really need is more capital. This is just as clear and definite as that the farmers in the above illustration needed more loanable capital. When the laborers begin to think in terms of the higher strategy, they will be trying to increase the quantity of capital. They can do this both by increasing their own savings and by encouraging saving on the part of other people. This is perfectly clear to any one who is not blinded by his primitive and inherited behaviorism. Many laborers as well as many highbrows are still blinded. Some of their self-appointed leaders are still leading them by appealing to their inherited attitude toward enemies. Most of the trade-union colleges that have thus far been started are led by people who still think in these primitive terms, and the policy of these colleges is to blind still further the laborers to the real economics of the situation.

In terms of the higher economic strategy, every encouragement of course should be given to laborers to organize their own banks and to run those banks as banks ought to be run, by safeguarding the capital of depositors and financing real, productive enterprises. But it is also to the interest of labor that other banks should be started to do the same thing. The more banks there are performing these two essential functions, the more capital there will be available for the financing of new and productive enterprises. If there is enough capital in the country and there are enough wise investors, no really productive enterprise will ever fail to secure adequate financial backing. When that happens, there will be so many productive enterprises in operation as to create a greatly increased demand for labor. This will put labor in a position of great strategic advantage. In other words, this is one of those cases where it is to the interest of labor to increase the number of its so-called enemies. In proportion as laborers learn to think in terms of economics rather than in terms of the cheap demagogics which is taught them by so many loquacious persons, they will begin to see the advantage of encouraging every possible accumulation of capital from every possible source.

III

What are some of the things that laborers should do in their own interest or that the friends of labor should try to do for them in terms of the higher strategy or more far-sighted wisdom? A constructive program in behalf of the laboring classes should, of course, include many things that we have already been doing in this country. A recognition of this fact may sound a little like the discovery that we have been talking prose all our lives without knowing it.

Yet we ought to be prepared for the belief that there has been some wisdom in our policy in this country in the past. The prosperity that has come to the laboring classes in America, as compared with that in other countries, would be an economic miracle if there were not some sound reasons for it; and miracles do not happen in the economic world.

First and foremost, there should be a keen discrimination between predatory and productive methods of getting a living. If we can bring it about that no one can ever get anything for himself without contributing an equal amount to some one else, we shall, of course, have achieved the motto, "He that would be great among you, let him be your servant." This merely means that success shall always be earned by giving an equivalent service. It means that the only avenue to success or greatness shall be the avenue of productivity or of usefulness. In so far as we succeed in this, we shall avoid the wasting of any manpower in nonproductive or nonserviceable activities. A hundred per cent. of our working power will be doing useful rather than useless things. This is the first condition of great prosperity in any country. The country that achieves this result must close down all unproductive industries in order that the productive industries may command a hundred per cent. of its man power. This means, among other things, a vastly greater quantity of useful products and of useful services than could possibly be produced or rendered in a country where a large percentage of its man power was commanded by or wasted in nonproductive or nonserviceable industries. This does not mean universal philanthropy. It means something very much better. It means that every one will be trying to achieve success, prosperity, or greatness for himself, but it also means that he will be trying to achieve that success for himself by trying to do the most useful thing he can find to do, expecting to be rewarded according to his usefulness. The country that can make every citizen feel that he will prosper in exact proportion as he contributes to the total prosperity, — such a country has achieved the first and fundamental condition of prosperity for all classes and occupations.

If we compare our own country with any other country on this basis, we shall find that we are not behind, but probably a little in advance of any of them in this respect. We have come more nearly to making every citizen feel that there is no limit to his success except the limit of his own usefulness than has any other country. In government, there is no office to which he may not aspire. In business, there is no limit to his fortune. In scholarship and other fields of useful achievements, there are no closed doors. In every field of useful work there is an open road to talent. On the other hand, we have restricted the useless and harmful fields more narrowly than has any other country. One need not be too priggish to mention, in this connection, the restrictions upon the manufacture and sale of narcotics, as well as of alcoholic drinks. Restrictions of this kind are and should be a factor in our prosperity, because they will save for our productive industries a lot of man power that formerly went, and in other countries still goes, into these useless or harmful industries.

Another item in a constructive labor program almost as fundamental as the one already described is a system of popular and universal education. Under such a system every young person has the opportunity to train himself for that position in which he can achieve the greatest usefulness to society, and — if the first item of the program is successfully carried out — the greatest prosperity for himself at the same time. That is to say, if we have achieved the first part of the program, so that every one may actually succeed according to his usefulness, then it follows as a matter of course that when a young man trains himself for the greatest success, he is of necessity training himself for the greatest usefulness. If every young person has the opportunity to train himself for the work that will bring him the greatest prosperity, he will, by that very fact, be training himself for the greatest possible usefulness. This part of the program is a positive factor, not only in promoting the general prosperity but in the diffusion of prosperity throughout the nation.

To begin with, if any young person is compelled

to do a less useful work when he might, had he had the proper training, have done a more useful work, something definite is subtracted from the possible prosperity of the country as a whole. The man is partially going to waste. He is not contributing as much as he might have contributed, had he been properly trained. So far as the general prosperity of the whole country is concerned, this is merely a matter of addition and subtraction. Improperly trained, his contribution is small. Properly trained, his contribution is greater. This applies to large numbers of people or nations as well as to individuals. If they all are improperly trained, their combined contributions to the total prosperity will be small. If they are all properly trained, their combined contributions to the total prosperity will be great.

As to the diffusion of prosperity, it will happen that if large numbers are improperly trained, and are compelled therefore to crowd into a few occupations that do not require training, those occupations will be overcrowded and poorly paid. If, however, every one is properly trained, he will have a wider choice of occupations and will therefore have the opportunity to avoid the poorly paid and seek the well-paid occupations. This would avoid the overcrowding as well as the undercrowding of any. When there is no longer an overcrowded occupation there will be no longer a poorly paid occupation.

Of course it should be understood that this system

of universal and popular education should apply not merely to the skilled manual trades, but that it should be carried to the very top of our social edifice. We should not be satisfied with merely training men and women for the skilled manual trades or even for the ordinary white-collar jobs. We should be prepared to train men to rise as high in the social and economic scale as their inherited capacity will permit them to rise. We should train employers, business managers, investors and inventors, as well as mechanicians, accountants and technicians. The aim, in other words, should be to redistribute our working population among occupations in such a way as to leave none overcrowded and none undercrowded. When this is achieved, there will be no great difference — all things considered — in the prosperity of different occupations.

In our educational policy, this country is not behind other countries, and is probably a little in advance of any of them, which helps to explain why we have achieved not only an enormous prosperity for the country as a whole, but a somewhat wider diffusion of prosperity than has any other. Others have achieved superior results in certain special fields, but no country has succeeded through its educational policy in redistributing its working population among all occupations so well as we.

Incidentally, prohibition is probably contributing something not only to the general prosperity but to the diffusion of prosperity as well. Addiction to alcoholic drinks does not tend to promote men from overcrowded to undercrowded occupations; it tends rather to demote them, or to hold them down and prevent their rising into the better paid occupations. In a country where alcoholic vice is widespread, many a man is compelled to do unskilled labor because he is not dependable enough to do more highly skilled or more responsible work. Nobody wants to ride behind a locomotive engineer who is addicted to drink. Nobody wants any one who is addicted to drink in a position of great responsibility. Those who are so addicted are fit only for positions of little responsibility. This tends to overcrowd such positions and to make lower wages in them. In this respect also, though there is still much to be achieved, we are not behind other countries and are probably a little in advance. One might observe, parenthetically, that the silliest argument that could possibly be uttered in behalf of labor is that the present prohibitory law is unfair to labor inasmuch as it permits the wealthy classes to buy bootleg liquor and makes it difficult for the laborers to get it. Those laborers who know their own interest are very thankful that this is true. In fact, it is rather fortunate for labor and for labor conditions that laborors as a class are not permitted to get it. Aside from the expense to themselves when a good part of their wages went for liquor, there was the tendency to overcrowd the unskilled occupations because of the inability of those addicted to drink to get into better paying occupations and relieve the overcrowding of the poorly paid occupations. Every constructive labor leader of the country realizes this and is frankly either for the strict enforcement of the prohibitory law or for some other measure that will reduce the evils of drink.

Another factor in the increase of general national prosperity and also in the wider diffusion of wealth has been the democratic idea that any useful occupation is respectable. The idea inherited from the militant type of society that business was less respectable than the profession of arms, politics, law, medicine or theology, has had no place in this country except among a small and negligible minority of sentimentalists. The attempt of radicals to associate the word *bourgeois* with all that is evil and repulsive is a mere perpetuation of that old aristocratic idea, inherited from a militant state of society. Men of violence have always despised men of peace. The *bourgeois* is merely the man of peace, — the man who tries to get what he wants either by producing it himself or by bargaining with other people. If you do not yourself produce what you want, there are only two ways of getting it from some one else. One is to take it without that person's consent; the other is to get it with his consent. The *bourgeois* method is to get it with the other man's consent. Now there are not many ways of getting something from a man with his consent. If he will not give it to you as a gift, you must manage to get it by an offer of something in return, either a product or a service. That involves a certain amount of bargaining. Those who are still thinking in terms of the old aristocratic tradition affect to despise bargaining and all that is associated with it; but after all, as pointed out before, there are not many ways of getting what you want, and the other ways are all a little less respectable, even, than bargaining.

In countries, however, where the older aristocratic tradition prevails, there is a positive preference on the part of men of unusual talent for other occupations than business. Where that is the case, business does not expand as rapidly as it might. One very necessary calling is depleted of men. In countries where there is no such aristocratic tradition, and where business gets its fair share of the highest talent of the country, business expands; there is a great deal of wealth produced and, what is more to the point, there is a great demand for labor. Where this great demand for labor exists, it results in one of two things: either laborers are imported from other countries to supply the demand; or, if they are not, wages for native laborers are high. That is to say, where the demand exists, if it is supplied from an inexhaustible foreign source, the only result is that large numbers of laborers are employed at low wages. Where it is not supplied from an inexhaustible foreign source, but can only be supplied by native laborers, not so many will be employed because there are not so many to be had, but those who are employed receive higher wages. There is no exception to this rule. The restriction of immigration has done more for American laborers than any other single piece of legislation of recent times. There is an acute need, however, for an extension of this restriction to immigrant laborers from Mexico. This and the vast amount of bootlegging in men, constitute the chief menace to American labor at the present time, and in addition they are rapidly creating a new race problem quite as serious as any that we have ever had.

Immigration from heaven, however, has about the same effect on the labor market as immigration from a foreign country. In other words, an inordinately high birth rate among laboring people tends to create a large supply of labor. A lower birth rate among laboring people means a smaller supply of labor in the next generation. If the demand for labor expands and the supply decreases because of a lower birth rate, wages go higher and higher, and prosperity is diffused. However, it is exceedingly important that the demand for labor be kept up, and one of the most important factors in increasing the demand for labor is the amount of real talent that goes into business. Where there are many smart business men, business expands; where there are only a few, or where business men generally are not very smart, business does not expand and there is little demand for labor.

We are sometimes misled into believing that a demand for commodities is all that is necessary to create a demand for manual labor. If manual labor were the only factor in the production of commodities, then a demand for commodities would itself create a demand for manual labor; but if it takes several kinds of labor to produce a commodity and one of them is missing, the demand for that commodity will not put the other laborers to work. For a simple illustration of this principle, suppose we consider the cranberry market. A demand for cranberry sauce is not a demand for cranberries, unless there is also a supply of sugar to mix with the cranberries in the making of cranberry sauce. If sugar is lacking, you might have millions of people clamoring for cranberry sauce, with plenty of money to pay for it, and yet not be able to sell a single barrel of cranberries. If you assume an abundant supply of sugar, then, if people begin to clamor for cranberry sauce, that will create an excellent market for cranberries. The same is true of labor of different kinds. There might be millions of people demanding cotton cloth and offering money for it, and there might be plenty of weavers ready to weave the yarn, yet all this demand for cloth would not put a single weaver to work unless there were farmers to grow cotton, spinners to spin it, and others to do the other kinds of work. If you assume, to begin with, that there were plenty of these other laborers, then the active demand for cloth would undoubtedly put the weavers to work by creating a demand for weavers. You might have multitudes of men capable of doing part of the work of manufacturing automobiles, but if there were none capable of doing the rest of the work — say the engineering or the organizing work — no demand for automobiles could be great enough to put a single manual laborer to work making them. But if all the necessary kinds of labor are present, then a demand for automobiles would put them all to work.

Now it happens that one of the scarcest factors in the expansion of any industry is organizing and directing talent. When this is scarce, it has the same effect on the demand for labor that a scarcity of sugar has on the demand for cranberries. When this is abundant, it has the same effect on the demand for labor that an abundance of sugar has on the demand for cranberries. A really constructive program in the interest of labor is one that would encourage the very smartest men in the country to go into business. The more Henry Fords there are in business, the more demand there will be for labor. The fewer Henry Fords there are, the less will be the demand for labor. Now suppose we lived under aristocratic traditions — as some old countries still do — under which a man of great talent would think that he was degrading himself if he went into business instead of into one of the more respectable occupations. You would naturally have fewer Henry Fords or other men of high talent in business. That would be bad for labor. But where democratic traditions prevail, and all useful occupations are regarded as equally respectable, where there is no prejudice against the *bourgeoisie*, where laborers themselves encourage men to go into business because they see that it will be good for labor if they do, — there you will find excellent conditions for labor, high wages and all the other things that laborers want, in great abundance.

Another factor in a constructive labor program is the increase in the supply of capital. If the laborers themselves are thrifty and careful to invest their savings in productive industry, that in itself helps to increase capital. If they encourage others also to save and invest, so that capital becomes very abundant and investors are watching for every possible opportunity to invest safely and productively, it is not likely that any really safe and productive industry will fail to receive proper financial backing. In a country where there is no thrift or little thrift, where there is very little capital seeking investment, only a few industries will ever be properly financed; therefore only a few will be in operation, and there will be little demand for labor. In a country where labor leaders write books on the fallacy of saving, where they talk about the evils of the capitalistic system, where they imagine that the way to increase wages is for everybody to consume up to his capacity, leaving no one with a surplus to invest in new inventions and new industries, in a country where the general attitude of labor is one of hostility to capital and capitalists, there will be comparatively little capital accumulated and little industrial expansion. Such labor leaders are doing injury to laborers and are not helping them. In a country, on the other hand, where labor leaders encourage thrift and wise investment among their people, where they encourage others of all classes to save and invest wisely, where they encourage the development of institutions for the accumulation and investment of savings, there all of the factors in industrial expansion will exist in great abundance. Capital will not be the limiting factor in the expansion of industry. If there is any limiting factor, it will be something else.

IV

A few years ago, some college students asked the writer what he thought was the largest field for social service now open in this country.[1] He replied, investment banking. The students were somewhat surprised at this answer; in fact, some of them were not able to see that investment banking was social

[1] *See* "The Economy of Human Energy", by the author. Page 203. The Macmillan Company, New York, 1924.

service at all; they thought it was money-making. They had been misled into accepting certain current notions about social service, which seemed to be that in order to perform social service, one must stop doing his regular work and begin doing something else. However, any useful work is social service. If it happens to be your regular work or the work by which you are getting your living, it is just as truly social service as if it were some other kind of work. The question was asked at a time when a number of fair-weather banks in Boston had suspended — banks that had accumulated large deposits by demagogical appeals, and then had wasted these resources in bad investments. Millions and millions of dollars of the hard-earned savings of people in poor or moderate circumstances were lost to them. What was more to the point, a great deal of man power had been hired to do things that were not worth doing, to erect buildings that were not needed, to start moving-picture shows in localities where people did not care to go.

Suppose those millions of dollars had been put in the hands of wise investors and had been spent to erect buildings where buildings were needed, shops and factories where they were needed, or, more especially, shops and factories with capable men at the head to insure their success. New England would have more industries running successfully than it now has. Because those millions of dollars of savings were wasted in bad investments, there are fewer industries running successfully than we might have had, there is less demand for labor than there might have been, and there are lower wages and more unemployment than we should have had.

If a large number of college graduates should study the problem of investment and become wise and sound investors, a great deal of that form of waste would be saved. The capital that is available for investment would be used to finance productive enterprises under capable men, and thus another factor in national prosperity and in the diffusion of wealth would be created.

In the accumulation of capital through the thrifty habits of the people and the wise management of business enterprises, we are not behind other countries and are ahead of most of them. Thus we have already another factor in the creation of general prosperity and the diffusion of that prosperity among all classes. In the development of wise investors we are not behind other countries, though there has been a vast amount of capital wasted by unwise investors; still, in spite of that, vast sums of capital in this country have succeeded in finding wise investment. Capital does not automatically find a wise investment; it finds it because it is directed by a wise investor.

There is one factor in the encouragement of thrift and the accumulation of capital in which we are probably behind every other country, — that is, in the regulation of wildcat schemes. A few States have already passed Blue-Sky laws which aim to check the promotion of fraudulent corporations and the selling of worthless stock to unsuspecting investors. The natural thrift and enterprise of our people have received many a setback because of losses incurred through the promotion of these worthless corporations. Men who have invested their hard-earned savings in enterprises that were foredoomed to failure cannot be blamed for feeling that hereafter they would better enjoy their money while they have it rather than invest it and lose it.

Of course some of this is involved in every investment. The most careful investor will sometimes lose his money, because nothing in this world is certain "except death and taxes." However, this does not excuse any State for permitting corporations to be formed for the sole purpose of selling stock to an unsuspecting public, with no idea of ever building a productive industry and no possibility of succeeding, even if the purpose were honest. The Blue-Sky laws at least succeed in weeding out most of these fraudulent promotions and reducing, in some slight degree, the hazard to the untrained investor. One reason why the French people are such famous investors is that fraudulent promotions are carefully repressed in that country. Any one with a small sum to invest is safeguarded in so far as government regulation can safeguard him. We have much yet to learn in this country on this subject.

The hazard of investing may be still further reduced by a more widespread knowledge regarding corporations and corporation methods. Even a sufficient knowledge of accounts to enable the average citizen to understand an ordinary bank statement would help. A sufficient knowledge to enable him to read intelligently a balance sheet would make for righteousness because it would make it a little more difficult for unrighteousness to flourish. We must look forward to a considerable increase in savings accumulations by the masses of the common people. This will furnish a rich harvest for fraudulent promoters unless they are hindered, first, by legal prohibitions in the way of Blue-Sky laws, and, in addition, by better information and more wisdom regarding investments on the part of the masses of the savers. The teaching of elementary economics in all our high schools, and the teaching of some of the simpler elements of bookkeeping and accounting in the grades, should be a part of the higher strategy of labor.

Even such extreme proposals as the guaranteeing of bank deposits are not to be hastily disapproved. There are difficulties in the administration of such a policy, but difficulties were made to be overcome. Because a thing is difficult is no reason for not doing it, if the result is really worth while. The guaranteeing of bank deposits may be expensive, but it will at least give savers more confidence than they now have in the safety of their deposits, and thus be a further aid to saving. This will be an important factor in the wider diffusion of prosperity, not simply because of the increased prosperity that comes directly to savers, but, as pointed out above, because of the increased wages that will come to laborers through the abundance of capital to finance every possible enterprise that shows promise of success.

Critics of the American people are always contradicting themselves, as is to be expected, and one of the current contradictions is the statement, on the one hand, that we are a nation of money grabbers, and on the other hand, that we are a nation of spendthrifts. As a matter of fact, we are neither. It is true that we seem to be rather successful in getting money, but no nationality parts with money as readily as we do. The average European or Asiatic who once gets his hands on a sum of money holds on to it more persistently than the average American. This would indicate to the analytical observer that our strenuosity is not ultimately the pursuit of money, but the pursuit of something else. There is many a game in which men seem to be feverishly accumulating counters of various kinds; and yet they are driven by the love of the game rather than by the love of the counters. Counters merely serve as a measure of a man's success in the game which he is playing. He desires to play the game well, and he desires also tangible evidences of his success in the game. Dollars, with us, are the counters in the greatest of all our games, namely, business.

How little we care for the money itself is evidenced by the ease with which we let go of it. There is no other country in which rich men are so liberal in the endowment of all educational and benevolent enterprises as this country. There is no other country in which they even throw money away so foolishly as some of our young inheritors of wealth are in the habit of doing. At the same time, it is true that there is no other country in which wise men give it away so wisely as our more seasoned money-makers are in the habit of doing. This should be a sufficient defence against the accusation that we are mere money-makers.

As to the accusation that we are a nation of spendthrifts, this can also be demonstrated to be false. It is true that we spend money rather freely; but the investor and saver spend money as truly as does the waster. To spend money for instruments of production is to spend it as truly as to spend it for articles of luxury. It stimulates the business of producing articles of production as truly as the other method of spending stimulates the business of producing the articles of luxury. It is true, of course, that hoarding is not characteristic of the American people; but because people do not hoard money, but insist on spending it pretty freely, this does not mean that they are a nation of spendthrifts. It may mean, and in this country it does mean, that they are a nation of investors. They are always ready to invest in any enterprise that shows signs of being productive. In some cases also, one must say with regret, they are ready to invest in enterprises that do not show the slightest sign of ever being productive. This readiness to invest in productive enterprises is one of the principal reasons why there are so many productive enterprises in this country, and that is one of the reasons why wages are so high here.

There is one sense and a rather important sense in which the American people are the most penurious in the world. They are penurious of time. No other country spends money so freely in order to save time as this country. There are some countries whose people will, on the average, spend a great deal of time in order to save a little money. We do precisely the opposite. We spend a great deal of money in order to save a little time. There may be some doubt as to which is the better form of parsimony. One can at least say that the country that is willing to spend a great deal of money in order to save time will probably have a great deal of money to spend; that is, it will be a very prosperous country. The fact that we are a country of this kind is one of the reasons why we are not only prosperous, but why there is a wide diffusion of prosperity among all classes. It should be a part of the higher strategy of labor to encourage this tendency.

V

Enough has been written, perhaps, to indicate that the general law of the higher strategy of labor consists primarily in increasing the number of the factors other than labor which are necessary to effective production, rather than in fighting against those other factors. Suppose, to turn again to our cranberry illustration, the cranberry growers should become incensed at the sugar producers and wage war against them. That would not be wise strategy on their part. If, on the other hand, they should take every possible measure to encourage sugar producers, when sugar was scarce, that would be wise strategy. In any economic situation the same principle will apply. If the demand for labor is limited by any limiting factor, and you can discover what that limiting factor is, and increase its supply, you will remedy the situation. If, in an agricultural community, there is plenty of labor but too little equipment, then equipment or capital is the limiting factor. What is needed is more capital in the form of farm equipment. The remedy is not to wage war upon capital and try to make it scarce. The remedy is to attract it. Herein lies the really constructive feature of the present Federal Farm-Loan system. A western farm mortgage is not very attractive to an eastern investor, because he does not know much about the farm or the farmer, and it would be expensive for him to find out. The problem for the western farmer is how to get that capital to move west. He cannot do this by waging war on capital in general. He has to do it by making that sort of an investment attractive to the easterner who has capital. He does this by substituting a standardized bond for a mortgage. The eastern investor can buy one of these standardized bonds without having to go to the trouble of inspecting a farm mortgage or the farm that is mortgaged. The machinery of the Farm-Loan system does the inspecting and certification, and thus relieves the eastern investor of that burden. This is a constructive way of meeting the situation and increasing the supply of capital in the western farm community where capital is the limiting factor. To have proceeded otherwise would have made matters worse rather than better.

If, as the result of this constructive labor program, the limiting factors are discovered, and wise measures are taken to increase the quantity of these limiting factors, the demand for labor will increase continuously and automatically, and make better conditions for labor in all respects. As a preliminary to this kind of a program, we must get over the notion that every time one man makes a dollar, somebody else must lose it. It is the aim of the present social system to make it impossible for any one to make a dollar without benefiting somebody else to an equal extent, and we are roughly succeeding in this aim. Progress lies in the direction of further perfection of this system. If it is to the advantage of western farmers to have more capital, it must be made to the interest of somebody to supply that capital. When somebody finds it to his interest to supply it, both gain. If it is made impossible for anybody to gain by supplying it, both lose, for the need will not be supplied except through charity, and the western farmer does not want charity.

The same is true of labor: it is to the interest of labor that the largest possible number of talented men should go into business; that these men should have available as large a supply of capital as possible; that there should be as many wise investors as possible who know how to pick the right kind of men to back with their investments.

In the last analysis, every investment is, in a rather strict sense, betting on a man. There are always dozens of men wanting to borrow money. It is perfectly certain that most of them would lose money if credit were extended to them. That is to say, they would use it so unwisely that they would never get enough back to pay the principal, to say nothing of interest. However, there are always a few who can use investible capital — that is, money — in such a way as to get from the things in which it is invested enough to repay the principal and a moderate rate of interest besides. It is the investor's business to pick out the right men as well as the right industries. It is to the interest of labor that the right men should be picked out. To bet on the wrong men — men who will spend the money and have nothing to show for it — does not expand industry or increase the permanent demand for labor. To bet on the right man who will invest productively is to expand industry and permanently increase the demand for labor.

It is to the interest of labor that capital shall increase as rapidly as possible. This will not only equip the existing number of laborers more abundantly, thus increasing their productive power; it will tend to lower the rate of interest. Labor will thus gain twice. It will gain in common with the country in general, through the increased productivity of industry; it will gain again by getting a larger percentage of this increased product. Labor leaders, who think in terms of this higher strategy, will be maneuvering in such a way as to increase all the other factors except labor, and, if possible, to decrease the supply of labor. During all the years of our industrial expansion, we have been increasing the demand for labor by the various methods and agencies mentioned above. We have only recently attempted a definite restriction in the supply of labor by shutting off the inexhaustible supplies from abroad.

This higher strategy of labor is beginning to be appreciated and is understood perfectly clearly by multitudes of laboring men. Unfortunately, only a few leaders who have this point of view have come to the top. The more vocal among them are still talking in terms of the fighting stage. No attempt can be made here to enumerate or classify leaders. One or two samples of the right sort will suffice. An excellent little pamphlet, "A Motorman's Message to You",[1] by John Henry Boyce, shows a perfectly clear and firm understanding of the correct principles. The article by Warren S. Stone, already referred to, not only shows a clear understanding of the same principle, it contains the following significant words regarding the place of the labor bank in this higher strategy:

That, however, is beside the question of an identity of interest between the employed and the employer. Until the labor bank came into being it was difficult to find a common ground. Labor and capital were islands, as the phrase goes, shouting at each other across seas of misunderstanding. Even though the workman owned his tools, and therefore was a capitalist; even though he owned his home, and therefore had wealth; even though he was in one sense a producer and in another a distinctly different person, a consumer, he still supposed that there was some essential difference between him and his employer. He thought a sharp line could be drawn between them. And the employer thought so too, in most instances. He thought the worker was getting

[1] Published in 1924, South Bend, Indiana.

as much as he could for as little as he could give. There was suspicion and hostility between them.

In the article entitled "Labor Banking in the United States", already referred to, Mr. Boeckel writes concerning the British view of labor banking in America:

Speaking of the fundamental changes in trade union policy, resulting from the establishment of labor financial institutions, Mr. John Murray, a former member of the British Parliament, writing in the London *Times*, says:

"The reformed trade unionism of America has set up new banks and acquired control of old ones, and it has made itself the predominant partner in many undertakings. To say that a new era has opened is the barest truth. It is not only that trade unionism has abandoned the old-fashioned policy of saving for fighting. It saves now to invest and for control. The motives of production are defeating the motives of antagonism."

The London *Economic Review*, after telling how British trade unionism in the past has "incessantly preached open war upon capital" and "accumulated and devoted funds to the furtherance of this project", says:

"It is a relief from the dullness of unpractical confiscatory proposals to be able to turn to America, where organized labor has resorted to different tactics in order to gain its share in the control of industry. In that country trade unions are financing industry and new enterprise, they are purchasing their power and control."

The London *Spectator*, arguing in the same vein, concludes that "there is nothing wild, nor anything economically unsound in the scheme" developed in America for securing a dominant share in control of industry for labor, through the strategic use of labor's money.

It has long been the ideal of certain farseeing people that it should be as legitimate an ambition of a farsighted business manager to pay high wages as to pay high dividends. There is no original or inherent reason why it should be considered a mark of good business management to pay high dividends rather than high wages; and yet, undoubtedly, there are more business managers who regard themselves as successful in proportion to the dividends they can pay than there are who regard themselves as successful in proportion to the wages they can pay. This is a temporary condition that need not exist indefinitely, though there is a very definite and specific reason for it while it does exist. So long as capital remained the limiting factor in industry, the capitalist was a more indispensable person than the laborer. So long as labor was so abundant as to be more or less superfluous, no business manager was ever likely to fail because of his inability to hire enough labor. He might very easily fail through his inability to secure capital. His chief worry was not how to get a sufficient supply of labor; it was how to get a sufficient supply of capital. A considerable number of laborers might refuse to work for him, but there were always plenty of others. If a considerable number of capitalists refused to let him have their capital or to invest in the securities which he had to offer, he would promptly go out of business. That is a necessary condition so long as labor is superabundant and capital is scarce. Reverse the conditions, make capital superabundant and labor scarce, and this result will automatically correct itself. When there is so much capital seeking investment that any number of capitalists may refuse to lend to a given enterprise or invest in its securities, there will always be plenty of others to take their places, provided it is a really productive enterprise. When labor becomes so scarce that the manager's chief worry is to know where he is going to get help, he will then be more anxious to placate labor than capital. His failure or success will depend more on his ability to pay satisfactory wages than on his ability to pay satisfactory dividends. It will therefore become his chief ambition to pay as high wages as possible, and his chief pride to have succeeded in paying high wages. This fact in itself will automatically give laborers a certain degree of control over industry, even though they do not themselves own the shares in the corporations which employ them. A wise and farseeing labor leader will work for the creation of these conditions, rather than try to grasp immediate control of industry, knowing that the power of labor will thereby be automatically increased. When the conditions are such that the withdrawal of capital will paralyze the industry, nothing that he can do will make the business manager more anxious to placate labor than to placate capital. If we can create the other conditions, the manager will be more anxious to placate labor than capital, and that without any terrorism. The mere fact that labor has become the limiting factor will impel him of his own volition to take the initiative by advertising to labor that it is his chief ambition to pay as high wages as possible. If he has been a success, he will, of his own initiative, point with pride to the fact that he has managed so efficiently as to be able to pay high wages. He will find it necessary to do this in order to attract enough laborers to his industry. He will not find it necessary to do this in order to attract enough capital. All he will have to do will be to pay a certain standard rate to capital, and that rate will become lower and lower as capital becomes more and more abundant.

CHAPTER EIGHT

What Capitalism Is and What It Does[1]

I

WHATEVER may be said against capitalism it has at least abolished famine in every country where it has been permitted to develop freely. That is more than can be said of any noncapitalistic system that ever existed. The worst that can be said against the capitalistic system is that it has not yet abolished inequality of wealth. Those inequalities which still persist, however, are not essential to the capitalistic system. In fact, where capitalism is given a chance to develop freely, unhampered by social and political obstacles, it tends to eliminate its own inequalities and secure not only great abundance for everybody, but to distribute the best things of life more evenly than any other system has ever succeeded in doing.

In spite of all the inequalities which persist under capitalism the masses of the people are better off under it than they have ever been under any other system. In fact, they are better fed, clothed, housed, and supplied with the adornments and embellishments of life than any but the rulers and a few heredi-

[1] *See* two articles by the author in the *Youth's Companion* entitled "What is Capitalism?" and "What Capitalism Does", in the issues of July 3, 1924 and July 24, 1924, respectively.

tary aristocrats in any noncapitalistic country. One needs only to be reminded that the United States is the most highly capitalistic country in the world to appreciate this fact. Next comes England, followed by France, Holland, Denmark, Germany, Italy.

It is an observed fact that laborers seldom migrate from a capitalistic to a noncapitalistic country, unless lured by free land or undeveloped mines, forests, or other natural resources. When these natural resources are once occupied and no longer free, the migration turns toward those places where capital has accumulated in largest quantities. That is where they find the best jobs, the highest wages, and the best living conditions. Except when lured by free natural resources, the migrations of laborers are away from the noncapitalistic countries. Either the laborers are very unwise in doing this or there is a sound reason why they should do so.

These reasons are perfectly clear to any one who understands what capitalism really is. The difficulty is that the word capitalism has been pronounced with such a wry face by so many persons. This has caused many of us to feel that it is necessarily bad. Those who feel that way about it have never really tried to understand it, but have tried, rather, to find new epithets to apply to it.

One difficulty in the way of a proper understanding of capitalism is the tendency to judge it by its superficial or temporary aspects rather than by its fundamental and permanent aspects. Strictly speaking, capitalism is not a system at all. It is merely a fact that grows out of the suppression of violence. Wherever violence is repressed, capital comes automatically into existence. Where violence is repressed, the man who has made a thing, or found it before any one else has gained possession of it, cannot be dispossessed without his consent. No government can repress violence without automatically creating property as a result. Of course, this is only the beginning of our present system of property. This germ that is created by the mere repression of violence has been cultivated and developed by many other acts of government. Rightful possession has to be defined; what constitutes valid possession, a valid transfer, a valid contract, and many other questions of like character, have to be determined by government through its courts before any modern system of property is complete. Nevertheless, property would exist, in a simple and undeveloped form, even if government did nothing in the world except repress all violence.

The repression of violence protects every one in his possessions. This protection at once transforms possession into property. Where violence is not repressed, one's possession of a thing is defended only by his own power. That is not property. Where violence is repressed, the possessor of a thing does not have to defend it himself. The government that represses violence protects it for him. The very act of repressing violence constitutes that protection. The so-called system of private property, therefore, is not a system in itself; it is a natural and unavoidable result of the repression of violence.

When the possessor of a thing cannot be dispossessed without his consent, any other person who wants it must contrive to get it, if he gets it at all, with the possessor's consent. Unless he can secure it as a gift he must offer something in exchange for it. There is no other way open to him. Exchange therefore grows up automatically and unavoidably along with property, whenever and wherever violence is repressed.

When one has come into possession of a thing, either as a gift or through peaceful and voluntary exchange, he is protected by the same rule against violence that protected the original possessor. He, in turn, cannot be dispossessed without his own consent. Any third person who wants it must get it from him — if he gets it at all — as the present possessor got it from its original possessor, either as a gift or in exchange for something, and so on. The repression of violence continues to protect every possessor who has himself come into possession without fraud or violence. This is the fundamental fact about property of any kind. It comes into existence as a necessary result of the repression of violence, and the revival of violence is the only thing that can possibly destroy it.

These possessions, which become property as soon as the possessor is protected through the repression of violence, are of two kinds. They are, first, objects of direct use and, second, objects of indirect use. Objects of the first class are sometimes called consumers' goods; those of the second class, producers' goods. Those of the first class are themselves used directly for the satisfaction of wants; those of the second class are used for the purpose of getting other things that will satisfy wants. Food, clothing, household furniture, pleasure vehicles — everything in fact which gives us direct satisfaction — belongs in the first class. Farms, tools, machines, shops, factories, railroads, — everything in fact that is used for the purpose of producing an income,— belongs in the second class.

Capital is the general name applied to all possessions of this second class. Wherever violence is repressed, men are protected in the possession of goods of this class as well as of the first class. Fundamentally, and in the strictest possible sense, that is the beginning of the so-called capitalistic system.

There are, however, several secondary features of the system, and these are the features which are more likely to attract the attention of the superficial student. When violence is effectively repressed, and every individual is, as a result, effectively protected in his possessions, the largest possible number of men have the largest possible encouragement to the accumulation of property. Where violence is not repressed, and no individual feels safe in his possessions, there is the smallest possible inducement to such accumulation. That is why it happens that desirable possessions accumulate most rapidly in those countries where violence is most effectively repressed.

This is especially true of the second class of possessions called capital, as described above. Food, clothing, and articles of personal adornment, satisfy immediate desires, and will be accumulated, at least in small quantities, where possessions are unsafe. Fighting men, savage chieftains, oriental despots, pugilists, thugs and highwaymen, who are able to defend their own property, are especially inclined to accumulate jewelry and other articles of personal adornment. Possessions of the second class, which are included under the name of capital, however, are of little or no immediate use. It takes time to get any advantage from having them. They have never been known to accumulate in a time or place where violence was not repressed. Men will not take the trouble to accumulate such things unless reasonably certain that they will not be robbed or dispossessed without their own consent. Give them safe conditions, however, and the farsighted ones will begin to accumulate them. A country that provides these safe conditions for a long time will always, in the course of time, be characterized by a large accumulation of producers' goods. This large accumulation is likely to attract attention, and certain superficial students will see no deeper. Not understanding the underlying conditions that made this large accumulation possible, they merely focus their attention upon the size of the accumulation, and call it the capitalistic system.

The safety which comes from the repression of violence not only encourages accumulation but also invention. In fact, mechanical inventions and accumulations of capital go together like the two blades of a pair of scissors. Neither is of much use without the other. Where there are no mechanical inventors, no matter how many savers or accumulators there are, such accumulations of wealth as are possible must largely be in the form of hoards of money, jewels and other consumers' goods rather than of producers' goods. Where there are no savers and accumulators, there is no one who is willing to invest labor or money in expensive machines. No matter how many inventive geniuses there may be, productive inventions will not be used. If conditions are so unsafe as to discourage savings and accumulations, goods whose uses extend over the distant future are not likely to be accumulated at all because every one is uncertain as to whether he will get the use of them or not. Mechanical inventions, especially of the larger and more productive sort, can seldom yield an immediate product sufficient to pay the cost. They must be kept for a long time before they will pay for themselves. In short, they are among the forms of accumulation which depend most closely upon safe conditions. No one will invest money or labor in such things unless he has confidence that they will not be taken away from him without his consent.

When conditions are safe, and remain so for a long time, not only are accumulations encouraged, but they tend to take on those forms that require a long time for their full utilization. The larger and more expensive instruments of production are of this kind. They have never accumulated where violence and uncertainty prevailed; they have, at least in recent times, accumulated wherever violence is suppressed and safety of possession takes the place of uncertainty.

The vast accumulation of machines and other expensive forms of capital that results from the permanent suppression of violence is very impressive. It seems to be one of the outstanding features of the present economic situation. It is not surprising, therefore, that a great deal of attention should be concentrated upon it, nor that they who concentrate their attention upon it should sometimes fail to see the underlying fact which produced it. The great tree is more impressive to the casual passer-by than the conditions which permitted it to grow.

These accumulations of powerful mechanisms,

however, do not constitute the real capitalistic system. They are merely the visible manifestations of it. The real system was created when possession was protected by the suppression of violence. Wherever that fact exists, the outward and visible manifestations of it, such as the accumulation of wealth in durable forms and the development of powerful engines of production, will come into existence. These things will not go out of existence until possession is no longer protected.

Under the system where the possessor is protected against violent dispossession, it may happen, and frequently does happen, that some individuals will accumulate more rapidly than others. In fact, some may accumulate rapidly and others not at all. Under conditions where violence prevails and no one is protected in his possession, the individual who possesses foresight and the individual who lacks it, will fare equally well or badly. Not foresight but the ability to defend oneself against violence is, under such conditions, the chief means to prosperity. Wherever such conditions prevail, differences in prosperity depend mainly upon differences in fighting power or power to defend one's own possessions. When men no longer need to defend themselves, the power of self-defense does not figure largely in their prosperity. Under these conditions, forethought becomes a factor in prosperity. These are the conditions that give foresight its opportunity. From this time forward, differences in prosperity are, at least in part, due to differences in forethought.

The existence of fraud or deception may still remain a factor unless the same power that defends the possessor against violence also defends him against fraud. When both fraud and violence are effectively repressed, industry and foresight, or general productive power, become the chief factors in prosperity. Differences in prosperity are based largely upon differences in the power to produce and in the foresight that leads to accumulation.

Even this situation is not free from danger. They who have, for any reason, failed to accumulate may envy those who have succeeded. Others may sympathize with the envious ones and invent apologies and excuses for them. If this envy grows strong enough, it is very likely to lead to acts of violence either by individuals or classes. Class war is especially dangerous and destructive of civilization. So long as the government succeeds in repressing violence, possessors remain safe in their possession. When, for any reason, the government fails to repress violence, possession ceases to be property. Possessions must then be defended by the prowess of their possessors or else the possessors will lose them to those who have the power to take by force what they want.

Sometimes the very engine, namely, government, that began by repressing violence becomes itself the engine of violence. Instead of defending the possessors, it uses its superior power to dispossess them. There is always danger of this if those who have not accumulated anything grow envious enough and numerous enough to gain control of the government. They may then use it as a means of taking accumulations away from those who accumulated them. The wealth thus taken away from its accumulators may then be disposed of in two ways. One is to give it to the nonaccumulators, the other is for the government to hold it and give the income derived from it to all without regard to the degree of foresight exercised by different individuals. Under these conditions, the foreseeing and the thoughtless fare alike. Foresight would not be rewarded at all because the individual would be given no opportunity to exercise it, or to accumulate the results of his foresight. If he tried to exercise it he would be dispossessed of his accumulations by the government. The very power which we now rely upon to protect us against being dispossessed without our consent would then be perverted to the performance of that which it was designed to repress.

It was pointed out earlier in this chapter that a highly capitalistic country, that is, a country where violence has been effectively repressed for a long time, and where accumulations have therefore been encouraged, always attracts laborers from noncapitalistic countries. They come because wages and other conditions are better than they were in their noncapitalistic homes. These good wages and good living conditions which attract immigrants also encourage the multiplication of thoughtless and thriftless people at home. There is, therefore, a strong probability that a considerable propertyless class will develop. It may become so large as to be dangerous. If it should be able to outvote the class of savers and accumulators, it may gain control of the government and use it as an engine for the dispossession of those who have managed to accumulate. The safety of modern civilization requires that these nonaccumulating classes shall be kept few in number.

The full development of the so-called capitalistic system will not be reached until practically every one has become a capitalist, that is, an owner or part owner of some of the instruments of production called capital. The suppression of violence took power out of the hands of those who were willing and able to prosper by the use of violence. This made it possible for those who were too gentle or too weak physically to profit by violence to prosper by means of their industry and foresight. When every one takes advantage of this opportunity, the full benefits of the suppression of violence will be realized. All real progress in the past has aimed in this direction, and all real progress in the future must lie in the same direction. No forcible leveling of the industrious and the idle is progressive; it is retrogressive.

Any forcible leveling of the thrifty and the thriftless, of the forethoughtful and the nonforethoughtful, is equally retrogressive.

The crisis of civilization is reached whenever civilized people face this question. When the nonaccumulators refuse to respect the laws for the repression of violence, and begin to take by violence what others have peacefully accumulated, conditions are bad enough. In so far as they succeed in defying the efforts of the government to preserve law and order, to that extent must civilization decline. Conditions are much worse, however, when the nonaccumulators, instead of resisting the government, become numerous enough to gain control of it and unscrupulous enough to use it as the means of violence, that is, as the agency for the forcible dispossession of the peaceful accumulators. This is vastly more destructive of civilization than merely resisting government.

II

A student from one of the islands of the Caribbean Sea, who is deeply interested in the prosperity of his people, states that conditions on his island have noticeably improved within his memory. Laborers are getting higher wages and every one has more of the good things of life than he had twenty years ago. Formerly many of the young people went to other countries to find work, but now they find as good jobs at home as abroad. He also tells me that the improvement came when some English and American capitalists invested about two million dollars in productive industries on the island. He naturally suspects that the investment of that capital and the development of those industries may have had something to do with the rise in wages and the increase in general prosperity. His reasoning is probably sound.

Several observations may be made regarding that situation. To begin with, the improvement was not due to the fact that it was English or American capital that was invested. It was because it was capital, and because it was wisely invested. If the capital had been accumulated and invested with equal wisdom by anybody else it would have done quite as much good. In fact, if it had been accumulated by the people on the island and invested as carefully and as wisely, it would probably have done even more good. But inasmuch as it had not been accumulated on the island, it was a fortunate thing for the laborers that it was brought in from the outside. The same may be said of the situation anywhere else. If the laborers would or could accumulate their own capital, and invest it as wisely as capitalists are now doing, it would be still better for the laborers; but until they are able to do it for themselves, it is a good thing for them that some one else does it. They will be able to accumulate their own capital out of the higher wages which they are now getting more easily than they could out of the low wages which they would be getting if no one else invested any capital in productive industries.

Another interesting fact about the changes which took place on that island is that they were on a relatively small scale. The establishment of a single large industry was sufficient to produce noticeable results. The improvement of conditions came so promptly after the establishment of the industry as to leave no doubt in the mind of any one that the establishment of the industry was a cause of the improvement in the conditions. In a great country like the United States, with such vast accumulations of capital already in existence and so many great industries already running, the results of investing a couple of millions of new capital and starting a new industry would not be so noticeable. They would seem like mere drops in a bucket. It is probable, however, that the investment of that much capital, and the development of a new industry of the same size, would employ as many men in this country as they did on that island. The only difference is that it would not make so great a difference in the larger labor market of this large country.

The essential thing to remember is that in any country, large or small, the investment of capital in a new and productive industry and the wise management of that industry always increase the demand for labor as well as its productivity. The increase in the demand for labor may merely increase the number employed and correspondingly decrease the number of the unemployed. If the workers of that island were only partially employed, as evidenced by the fact that many of them had to emigrate to find jobs, and the new industry enabled them all to find employment at home, there was a definite gain to laborers as a whole, even though the rate of wages had not risen at all. On the other hand, the increase in the demand for labor may do much more than reduce the number of the unemployed. It may increase the wages of those who were already employed. It might even attract laborers from other islands and create an immigration problem instead of an emigration problem on the island where the improvement had taken place. If laborers from other islands, where there was unemployment, came in large numbers to this island where there is an increasing demand for labor, there is a gain to the laborers of the world, even though the laborers already on the island get no higher wages than before.

This, however, could hardly happen. If there were so little demand for labor on the island as to make it impossible for the existing supply of labor to find employment, the almost necessary result would be low wages even for those who were employed. If, as a result of the change, the demand for labor should afterwards exceed the local supply, the almost necessary result would be a rise of wages for those already on the island. The only effects of immigration to the island would be, first, to stop the rise of wages and prevent them from rising as far as they would if there were no immigration; and, second, to enable a larger number of laborers to earn wages at the existing rate.

It is not improbable that some citizen of that island, less enlightened than my student friend, may even now be contending that this investment of capital is an injury to the island or to the laborers who live there. He could point to the money that goes out of the island to pay interest to the investors, and he could maintain that these interest payments are just so much subtracted from the income of the people of the island, or of the laborers who work in the industry where the capital is invested. He would, if he were not quite honest, fail to point out that the total income of the islanders has so increased as to enable them to pay the interest and still have more left for themselves than they would otherwise have had, or that the capitalists had added more to than they were subtracting from the total income of the island, or that this is one of those numerous cases where both parties to a business arrangement gain something and one does not necessarily lose all that the other gains.

It is, of course, true, as suggested above, that if the people of the island had accumulated their own capital and had invested it as wisely as these foreign capitalists did, they would be still better off than they are now. That is to say, the wise investment of their own capital would have raised their own wages quite as much as the investment of foreign capital did, and they would now be receiving interest in addition to their high wages. This, however, in no way obscures the fact that their wages were raised through the investment of this foreign capital, and that, since they did not have capital of their own to invest, it was a good thing for them that foreign capital had come in.

Our own laborers in this country are frequently told that capitalists are robbing them of their wages. In proof of this, it is pointed out that a part of the product of the industries in which laborers are employed goes to pay interest on capital owned by others. This is not a thoroughly ingenuous argument, because it does not point out to the laborers how much more productive the industry is because of the wise investment of capital than it would otherwise be; nor that in spite of the interest charges, the laborers receive more wages than they could possibly receive if large sums of capital had not been wisely invested in the industry. Of course it is true of them, as of the islanders, that if they had themselves accumulated their own capital and had invested it in their own industry as wisely as others had done, their wages would be quite as high as they now are and they would be receiving interest besides. They would be both laborers and capitalists and getting both incomes. But inasmuch as they had not accumulated their own capital, it is a good thing for them that some one else did. They are at least getting better wages than they would otherwise be getting.

Even those who inveigh against capitalism and deny that the capitalist does any good, or earns anything for himself when he invests capital in a productive industry, are compelled to change their tune when they face a practical situation. Russian communism was not strictly a revolt against Czarism, since Czarism had already been overthrown. It purported to be a revolt against capitalism and, like all communism, was based partly upon the proposition that labor produces all wealth and that, therefore, whatever the capitalist gets is necessarily just so much subtracted from wages. The Russian Communists are now clamoring for capital and trying to borrow it from the outside world. Even the expedient of issuing unlimited money does not supply capital for the very simple and obvious reason that money is not capital. Capital consists of tools, machines, buildings and everything else of a material nature used in production except land. Money is only a means of purchasing such things. When the money you issue will not purchase them it does you no good.

If labor produces all wealth, Russia ought to be rich. She has plenty of labor. But she now realizes that she needs capital also. There are only two ways of getting it. One is to accumulate it and the other is to borrow it. If she can accumulate it she will not need to pay interest to foreign capitalists; yet she is trying to borrow it. Why does she not accumulate it herself? She may have to do so, but it will be a slow process. Borrowing would be much quicker. With very little capital to start with, her industries are not very productive. When her industries are not very productive, wages must necessarily be low. Out of low wages it is difficult to save and invest capital, therefore it will be a slow and painful process to accumulate her own capital. When she does, it will raise wages just as much as though that capital were borrowed, and she will not have to pay interest to foreigners. But, however she gets it, she must have more capital before she can have good wages.

If she can borrow capital at once and equip her industries with machinery and all that is needed, then her industries will be much more productive than they now are. This equipment will enable her industries to pay higher wages than they can possibly pay without it. Out of these higher wages it will be easier to save and accumulate capital. When her people do this, they can pay off their foreign debts and own their own capital. They can thus own their own capital much sooner and with less painful effort by borrowing than by not borrowing. For this advantage they can well afford to pay interest to foreign lenders. They will enjoy more prosperity while paying interest, and they will become their own capitalists sooner than if they fail to borrow capital. Foreign lenders, however, must not be blamed for being a little cautious about lending to people who profess, in one breath, to disbelieve in all interest payments while, in the next breath, they profess to be willing to pay interest for much-needed capital. It is not improbable that after they get the capital, some one will point out that it is unnecessary to continue paying interest to foreign lenders.

In the efforts of the Russian government to borrow capital in this country, their agents make use of some very sound economic arguments. They tell us that the Russian workmen have land and raw material, but that they need capital and are willing to pay for it. We are urged to help them to help themselves. We are reminded that it is very much better to invest capital in Russia so as to give jobs to Russians than it is to give them charity. This is undoubtedly a sound argument. It is a pity that it is not convincing both to themselves and all others who oppose capitalism. The reason it is not convincing is that it is so directly contrary to the whole theory and practice of communism. In order to help the Russian laborer to help himself, the government is compelled to deny communism and to accept capitalism completely, or without any material qualification.

What capitalism does is to equip laborers with

tools, machines, buildings, raw materials and whatever else is necessary for efficient production. Before the days of mechanical inventions, when tools were simple and inexpensive, it did not take much capital to equip a given number of laborers. Now it takes a very large quantity. That is the only essential change which has taken place in the nature of capitalism. Now, no group of laborers could hope to earn good wages unless they were supplied, from some source, with a very expensive equipment. If they equip themselves, they are then their own capitalists.

That is a desirable end toward which to work, but it should be pursued by peaceable means. The workers in a shoe factory, for example, must have buildings, machines, and leather that were made by other laborers. Those other laborers must be paid for their products. If the shoemakers themselves buy the buildings, machines, and leather, they become, by so doing, their own capitalists. If some third group buys the buildings, machines, and leather, paying the laborers who made them, then the members of this third group become the capitalists in the shoe industry. There would seem to be no better reason for dispossessing them without their consent than for dispossessing the original producers. So long as the owners of the equipment acquire their ownership by peaceful purchase, we have capitalism, whether the purchasers be the laborers themselves or some one else. Enlightened governments not only recognize the right of the maker of a thing to own it, but also an equal right on the part of the purchaser of it.

Some think that the government should own all the capital and see that laborers are equipped with the necessary buildings, machines, raw materials, etc., and pay the laborers their wages. In other words, they think that the government should do exactly what capitalists are now doing. Yet, instead of acknowledging the important part that capitalists are now playing in industry, they indulge in general denunciations of capitalists and capitalism, even asserting that capitalists are a parasitic class. If so, why should they want the government to do exactly what capitalists are now doing? Again, they say that capital, instead of being an aid in production, is merely a means of robbing the laborer. If that is all it does, why should the government own it?

If capital is not an aid in production but only a means of robbing the laborers, wages and prosperity should have declined on the island of our student friend after the new fund of capital came in. Instead of that, they rose. There is evidently something wrong with the theory that capital is parasitic. If capitalists were parasites and capital a means of extortion, we ought to find prosperity everywhere declining in proportion as capitalists and capital increase. It does the opposite. If laborers really believe that capitalists are robbing them by means of capital, we should expect them to emigrate from places where capital is accumulating and seek places where it is not. Instead, they do the opposite. Here are some hard nuts for those to crack who deny the usefulness of capital and capitalists.

CHAPTER NINE

Some Consequences of a Balanced Economic System

I

THE most revolutionary idea ever injected into economic discussion is that of a balanced economic system. A balanced economic system is one in which all factors of production are combined in such proportions as will yield the most satisfactory results, and yield them automatically. To begin with, this idea is so new when stated in its logical entirety, as to be incomprehensible to any except those who have the patience to ponder it. Most men have their minds made up and cannot be induced to give this idea the full consideration that it merits. In the next place, its consequences are so alluring and so vast in their scope as to be unbelievable to those who have become somewhat pessimistic as to social amelioration. The man who has to be shown, the hard-headed, incredulous type of man, is the backbone of modern democracy and the safeguard of our institutions. He is suspicious of anything that promises too much. That is why he never goes in for socialism, communism or any of the thousand other isms that are dinned in his ears. The writer appreciates the value of such men and, also, the difficulty of convincing them even when one has the truth on one's side. Nevertheless, they are the only people really worth convincing.

Another difficulty is the extreme simplicity of the proposal. It seems incredible that so simple a method can produce such vast and extensive results. These are comparable with the results of a balanced diet upon health, when the dietitian knows all the elements of a balanced diet. It is simple in the sense that it is merely the extensive application of familiar, everyday principles which every one recognizes in their detailed applications, and every one uses somewhere in his business. The sole difficulty is in the synthesis, in the attempt to bring together into one general policy all that is known about balancing the ingredients, the factors and the forces that have to be balanced in every undertaking in any field whatever.

Where several things have to be combined in order to get a certain result, the question of the ratio in which they combine most satisfactorily can never be without interest. Wherever they are actually combined in satisfactory ratios there is said to be a balance among them. Thus, the scientific dietitians and the cattle feeders speak of a balanced ration when the nutritive elements are combined in such ratios as to secure the most satisfactory results. Soil chemists and farmers speak of a balanced soil when the different elements of plant growth are combined in such ratios as will give the maximum productivity. Not enough attention has been given to the necessity of carrying this idea of balance throughout the whole nation, or the whole industrial system, balancing every industry against every other, and every element or factor in every industry against every other. The statesman and the economist should be as definitely interested in this larger problem of balance as the various experts already named are in their own special problems of balance.

Of course the dietitian, the cattle feeder, or the soil chemist has in each case a special purpose which he wishes to accomplish. Such a balance as will enable him to accomplish that purpose is to him a satisfactory balance. Similarly, the statesman or the economist must know what he wishes to accomplish before he can decide upon a satisfactory balance. For purposes of this discussion, it will be assumed that each wishes to achieve a wide diffusion of wealth, amounting to practical equality of prosperity among all classes and occupations. Any balance of the factors in national life that will automatically achieve this result will be called a satisfactory balance.

Some idea as to what is meant by a satisfactory balance may be reached by considering first, something that may be called an unsatisfactory balance. Some writers have referred rather vaguely to a static condition in economics. Others have improved upon this idea by speaking of an equilibrium of supply and demand. There is said to be an equilibrium of supply and demand when the quantity of a given commodity for sale at a given price is exactly equal to the amount that would be bought at that price, so that there are no sellers with unsold supplies or buyers willing to pay the price but unable to get any of the commodity. The price that will bring about such an equilibrium is said to be an equilibrium price. On the labor market, for example, there may be said to be an equilibrium of the demand for and the supply of a given kind of labor when every laborer of that class can get work, and every employer who wants help can get it. The wage that would attract exactly the number of laborers that employers were willing to hire would be the equilibrium wage. There would be no laborers willing to work for that wage and unable to get work, and no employers willing to pay it and unable to get help.

This state of equilibrium on the labor market would not be a satisfactory balance unless the equilibrium wage were high enough to give the wage workers a degree of prosperity comparable with every other class. To be more specific, the wages of a certain kind of labor may be an equilibrium wage, in that it induces as many men to offer themselves for hire as employers care to hire, and yet the price may be so low as to leave the laborers exceedingly poor. A low standard of living among them may make them perfectly willing to reproduce their kind in sufficient numbers to keep up the labor supply, even at the low wages; there may be, in some part of the world, a reservoir of cheap labor, which will be glad to migrate in order to get the low wages offered; the educational system may be so ineffective that the children of the poor have no choice other than to accept employment in the poorly paid occupation; or some of the other factors of production may be so scarce as to reduce the opportunities for the productive use of this class of labor. In any or all of these cases, the equilibrium of the supply of and the demand for the kind of labor in question may be maintained indefinitely, in spite of the fact that its wages are unsatisfactory from the social point of view.

Even in this case, whatever the wages are or are not, there must be an equilibrium wage. To decree otherwise would create worse evils than it would cure. To decree higher wages for all comers would encourage still earlier marriages and larger families, or it would stimulate still greater immigration, or in some other way induce larger numbers to offer themselves for hire in the industries in question. At the same time it would not induce employers to hire so many as at the lower wages. The result would be wholesale unemployment. While a certain number of laborers would gain a slight advantage through the rise in wages, yet industry would either be cluttered up by a great surplus of such laborers who would get in one another's way, or some of them would suffer the great disadvantage of failing to get employment at all. To decree higher wages, in such a case, is to apply the remedy to the symptom of the disease and not to the cause.

If, however, the supply of labor of the grade in question could be materially reduced, or the opportunities for employment increased, the situation would automatically cure itself. The supply of labor could be decreased, either by raising the standard of living, so that laborers would not be willing to reproduce their kind and keep up the supply of labor on so low a wage, by the restriction of the immigration of that grade of labor; or by an improved system of popular education so that the children of those laborers already in the overcrowded occupation could have the opportunity of choosing a less crowded and better paid occupation. The demand for labor could be increased by encouraging the expansion of industry, by encouraging as many talented men as possible to go into business, by training men for the higher business positions, or by encouraging the accumulation of capital. The equilibrium price of labor would then rise. That is to say, it would then take a higher wage to induce as many men to offer themselves for hire as employers would be willing to hire. We should still have an equilibrium wage, and at the same time a wage that would be more satisfactory from every social point of view.

In short, we should then be applying our remedy to the cause rather than to the symptom of the disease.

A possible way out of the difficulties, certain to arise from the attempt to apply the remedy to the symptom rather than the cause, that is, of trying to decree high wages before readjusting the balance, would be to decree the high wages first and then reduce the supply of labor afterward. This could be done, first, by admitting only as many immigrant laborers of the grade in question as could get work at the higher wage; second, by permitting only as many native-born laborers to work as could get work at the higher wages, encouraging the surplus to emigrate, to go to the almshouse, or to go to school to learn a new trade in which wages were better; or third, by increasing the other factors, such as land, capital, and other kinds of labor needed to balance up the oversupply of the kind of labor in question. The decree of high wages might thus be made effective by balancing up the labor market. It should be remembered, however, that if the labor market had been balanced up first, the decree would have been unnecessary, because there would have been high wages anyway.

II

By a balanced industrial system[1] is meant a system in which every essential industrial function

[1] For an elaboration of this, *see* the author's "Principles of National Economy", chapter XVII. Ginn and Company, Boston, 1921.

is as well and as adequately performed and as well paid, all things considered, as every other. This means a system in which it is as important that one factor of production be increased as any other factor. If in a given factory there are so many men doing one kind of work, and so few doing another kind, that a larger gross product would result if one man could be transferred from the one kind of labor into the other kind, the industry is not well balanced. Another way of stating it would be to say that if it would add more to the gross product if one more man could be added to one part of the working force than if one more man were added to another part of the working force, then the working force is not well balanced. It is this perception of the greater desirability of having one more man rather than one less man in one part of the force than in another part that will induce the manager to pay higher wages to the one part of the force than to the other. To be sure, if he can get one kind of labor cheaper than another, that will be a sufficient reason why he should hire more of the one kind than of the other. The price or wages in each class is a means of producing an equilibrium of demand and supply in each case; but, as already shown, the equilibrium of demand and supply which results from this kind of price adjustment is not a true economic balance from the point of view of one who desires equality of prosperity among occupations.

To use more technical language, there can be no true economic balance unless the marginal productivity of labor is approximately the same in each and every occupation. When the marginal productivity is the same in different occupations, the equilibrium wage in the different occupations will be approximately the same. There is thus an equilibrium of demand and supply, but the forces determining that equilibrium are such as to give approximately equal incomes to every class of workers, not even excepting managerial and professional workers.

Care has been taken to speak of different occupations or different classes of workers, and no statement has yet been made regarding the wages of individual workers in the same occupation. So long as one occupation is as remunerative as any other, or one class of laborers as well paid as any other, there may be said to be an equilibrium or balance among occupations. If, as has been shown before, within the same occupation there are differences in strength, skill, intelligence, or general efficiency, that is an individual affair which no social policy can affect. If one bricklayer can lay twice as many bricks as another, there is an undoubted difference in productivity that no social or economic law can affect or modify. But if brick masons are neither more nor less numerous in proportion to the need for them than are the members of any other trade or profession, then brick masons as a class should be neither more nor less prosperous than any other class, trade, or profession. There might still be as great differences in the prosperity of different individual brick masons as between the individual members of any trade or profession.

This is a matter of some importance, because it seems to be a law, or at least a general tendency, for individual differences to count for more as you proceed from the less skilled to the more skilled occupations. The differences in the productivity and the value of individual ditch diggers, while considerable, is by no means so great as among skilled laborers, and these differences, of course, are greatest of all in the intellectual and artistic callings. Since we usually focus our attention upon the individuals who are conspicuous successes in these callings, rather than upon the numerous failures, we are likely to get exaggerated notions of the differences in the prosperity of different occupations. However, such differences of prosperity as exist between different occupations are due to a lack of balance in the industrial system.

Since equality of prosperity is the first sign or symptom of a properly balanced industrial system, as inequality is of an unbalanced system, the first and most conspicuous result of a balanced system has already been stated. It is the approximate equality of prosperity as between different industrial classes or occupational groups. But this does not exhaust the catalogue of results.

Incidentally, and as a part of the equalizing process, there would be an equalizing of the bargaining power of different groups, notably that of the capitalists and the laborers. Freedom to bargain for oneself is sometimes said to mean the freedom to starve. That can be true only when the industrial system is unbalanced. We have frequently been regaled with a list of reasons why the capitalist is always and necessarily at an advantage in the bargaining process. Observation does not show that the capitalist as such has any advantage except when labor is oversupplied. When there is a dearth of labor and a plethora of capital the advantage is invariably on the other side. When men are hunting for jobs and employers are not hunting for men, but merely taking their pick among the men who are applying, the advantage is obviously on the side of the employer; and for no obscure or occult reason. When, however, employers are hunting for men and men are not hunting for jobs, but only taking their pick among the jobs that are offered, the advantage is just as obviously on the side of the laborer, and for the same reason that it was on the side of the employer under the other conditions.

A by-product of this balanced condition is that laborers need none of those special aids or helps in bargaining that most of us have tolerated, and some have advocated in the past. With bargaining power equalized, as it would be under a properly balanced industrial system, the individual of whatever class, trade, or occupation can be his own master and make his own arrangements, bargains, or voluntary agreements with other individuals, retaining his freedom and prospering under it. Under such conditions freedom would never mean the freedom to starve. No one would need to surrender his freedom in order to prosper, nor his prosperity in order to be free. He could have both freedom and prosperity — two good things — and it is certainly better to have both than either one without the other.

Another result would be to make most of our social legislation unnecessary. Neither the laborer nor anybody else would need the State or any paternalistic organization to safeguard his interest beyond protecting him against violence and fraud. When every man can take his pick among several jobs, the job that provides the best working conditions would attract him, and the competition of employers for men would compel them to offer satisfactory conditions in order to get and hold an adequate number of laborers.

One of the most important of all the results would be the participation of labor in the management of industry, on a purely voluntary basis, without threats, or any kind of compulsion on its part. If you were about to start a business enterprise and were casting about for the different factors of production, you would offer special terms to that factor which was hardest to get. If you discovered that there was an abundance of labor looking for jobs, and felt certain that as soon as you were ready to use labor, there would be plenty of laborers on hand asking you for jobs, you would not worry on that score. You would give the problem of getting help no second thought. If, on the other hand, you found that capital was not forthcoming in the same way, that capitalists were not thrusting capital upon you, that they all had numerous other uses for their capital and would not let you have it unless you offered better terms than other opportunities were offering, you would be compelled to worry somewhat over the question of capital. In fact, you would go to those who had it, and offer them terms, or accept such terms as they laid down. They would be in a position to demand some voice in the control of your business, and you would be compelled to grant their demand. Now, if this condition could be reversed, or only considerably changed in the direction of a better balance, you would be just as likely to give the laborers as the capitalists a voice in the management of the business.

If, to take an extreme case, there were so much capital seeking investment as to make you certain that as soon as you could use it some one would be on hand to offer it to you, but if labor were so scarce and hard to find as to make you feel uncertain whether you could get any or not, your anxiety would be on the side of labor and not on the side of capital. You would have to go to laborers and persuade them to take your job rather than some others that were open to them. Under such circumstances you would have to accept their terms, even if they included a voice in the management of the business.

Even now it sometimes happens that the enterpriser needs some special kind of labor, technically trained or possessing special skill, which is very hard to find. Men possessing this skill are not looking for jobs; they all have good jobs, with others waiting for them. When your enterpriser goes after such men he is very likely to offer them whatever they demand, even though it be a voice in the management of the business. He will do the same with any and every kind of labor that is scarce enough.

The indispensable man can generally get what he wants; the superfluous man must take what he can get. When a man is as nearly indispensable in one occupation as in any other, or no more nearly superfluous in one than in any other, — in short, when there is an industrial balance, power as well as prosperity will be diffused.

That power as well as prosperity comes to those who follow an occupation where workers are scarce and hard to find can be shown by hundreds of illustrations, ranging all the way from cooks to capitalists. That neither power nor prosperity comes to those who follow an occupation where men are abundant and easy to find can be shown by equal numbers of illustrations, ranging all the way from ribbon clerks to preachers.

III

One of the means of creating a balanced industrial system is undoubtedly an effective system of popular education. One of its chief functions, in an unbalanced industrial system, is to train people so that they may avoid the overcrowded and poorly paid occupations and enter the uncrowded and well-paid occupations. Every time a man is so trained, there is one less man who must work in an unskilled and overcrowded occupation, and one more man who can enter a skilled or learned occupation. Every such case helps to create a proper balance and the more such cases there are the more speedily will such a balance be created.

Lest some one object that even the skilled and learned occupations are as badly overcrowded as the unskilled manual trades, let me point out again how easily one may be deceived by the equilibrium of demand and supply, as commonly interpreted and as brought about by the equilibrium price. If one has the preconceived idea that ten thousand a year is about a proper income for a business or a professional man, whereas two thousand a year is quite enough for an unskilled laborer, one may easily reach a false conclusion. When one finds that it is about as hard for a business or professional man to get an income of ten thousand as it is for an unskilled laborer to get two thousand, one may conclude that business and the professions are as badly overcrowded as are the unskilled trades. This false conclusion is based on the false assumption that any income is proper for one class that is not equally proper for any other class, barring differences in the cost of acquiring the necessary skill. When we get rid of this false assumption we shall see that two occupations are not equally overcrowded until prosperity is equalized between the two. To equalize prosperity, however, would require that there should be enough difference in incomes during the working years to compensate for the difference in the cost, in time and money, of acquiring the necessary skill. If the differences of income are greater than this it argues that the occupation with the smaller incomes is more overcrowded than the one with the larger incomes.

One of the most far-reaching and surprising results of a balanced industrial system is its effect upon our system of education. One of the principal functions — some would call it the principal function — of our present system of popular education is to train pupils for more remunerative occupations than they could enter if they were not educated. Precisely the same thing may be said in another way. One of the main purposes of a system of popular education is to train pupils to be more useful than they could be without education. Generally, with some exceptions, the more useful the person the more he is paid. In the past, this has meant, in many cases, training pupils for more remunerative or more useful work than their parents, who were uneducated, could do. With an oversupply of manual labor, it was, of course, neither necessary nor desirable to educate men for this kind of work. It was necessary to educate them for the occupations where more men were needed because they were scarce, and the best single piece of evidence to show that men were scarce in any useful occupation was the income which that occupation promised.

When every child is so trained that by the time he grows up he has a choice of several occupations, and when in addition he is well informed or well advised, he will avoid any occupation that is overcrowded and underpaid and seek one where conditions are better. The wider the choice of occupations open to each young person, and the better he is advised, the more general becomes this avoidance of the overcrowded and the seeking of the uncrowded occupations. The logical extreme of this tendency would be so to distribute our population occupationally, as to leave no occupation more overcrowded or underpaid than any other. If our educational system could function so perfectly as that, it would create for us such a state of balance as would equalize prosperity among all occupations. What would there then be left for our educational system to accomplish?

What would happen to our educational system after the industrial system was once balanced up? It is obvious that one of its functions, namely, that of balancing up the system, would have been performed, and to that extent it would seem to have made itself unnecessary. On the other hand, it would be truer to say that it would then have been relieved of the burden of having to perform one of its functions and would be free to devote its whole energy to the performance of the remaining functions. However, the necessity of preserving the balance already achieved, by counteracting any tendency to throw it out of balance, would still remain. In general, however, the problem of redistributing our population, by training numbers of the rising generation to do more remunerative kinds of work than their fathers had done, without very much regard to their individual capacities, would not be so very acute, because there would be no occupations that were more remunerative. Educators could then consider the individual aptitudes of individual pupils, without much regard to the differences in the market values of different aptitudes, since there would be no great differences in the market values of different aptitudes. Under the unbalanced condition which most of us know, if a pupil shows a special aptitude for a kind of work which is being overdone and poorly paid, to train the pupil for that work would be to condemn him to poverty, and no conscientious educator would care to do that. He must, in fact, train the pupil for a kind of work which is reasonably well paid, and for which the pupil shows some aptitude, even though it be not the kind of work for which he shows the greatest aptitude. When all kinds of useful work are well paid, the educator's problem is greatly simplified.

To summarize, it is the opinion of the present writer that a balanced industrial system would produce four important results: First, it would equalize prosperity among different occupations, though not among different individuals within the same occupation. Second, it would equalize bargaining power as between classes of bargainers, though individual differences in bargaining power would remain. Third, it would tend to diffuse power as well as prosperity among all classes, giving those who follow one trade or occupation approximately as much control over business as would be possessed by those who follow any other occupation. Fourth, it would work a profound change in our educational system by relieving it of what is now one of its chief functions, namely, that of redistributing our population occupationally by training men to avoid the overcrowded and to seek the uncrowded occupations.

The significant thing about it all, however, is that all these results would be achieved without disturbing the institution of free contract or voluntary agreement, as a basis of economic action, which is the fundamental characteristic of all free peoples, and against which most of the revolutionary propaganda of the day is being launched. Not many would regret any of these consequences. There are others, however, that would not be so welcome, even to people who apply to themselves such terms as "socially minded", "progressive", or "sympathetic."

The vast improvement in the condition of the laboring classes that would undoubtedly follow from a balanced economic system, might take any one of several forms. During the preliminary stages, it might or might not take the form of decreased unemployment. Unemployment can be created by trying to force actual wages higher than the equilibrium wages, as defined earlier in this chapter. If, for example, the wages of coal miners are made so high as to attract too many men into that occupation, there will necessarily be unemployment. That is, if half the coal miners working full time, or all of them working half time, can mine as much coal as the public will buy at the necessarily high price, there will necessarily be unemployment. That condition could only be cured by reducing the numbers of coal miners, or increasing the consumption of coal. The same observation might apply to any industry.

A certain amount of unemployment always results from maladaptation. Some one thinks he can act for the movies, sing for the opera, repair automobiles, or do any of a thousand difficult kinds of work. If he is not fitted for the work he wants to do he will probably be unemployed until he finds his proper place in our economic system. Again, there is the terrible problem of the unemployable — the permanent misfits in our economic system. Even an economic system so well balanced as to give equal prosperity to every occupation would not necessarily take care of all these misfits; neither would any other economic system.

IV

There are other things about a well-balanced economic system that would be unwelcome to those who find themselves so very comfortable at present. It is very comfortable to have a train of loyal servants attached to one's household who will stick by one through thick and thin and relieve one of all drudgery. There is also something splendid in the loyalty of the old-fashioned servant, on the one hand, and in the feeling of responsibility on the part of the old-fashioned master, on the other hand. When that old relationship passes completely away, the world will lose something, although something much better may be gained in its stead. The contrast between the paternal and the commercial relationship is well expressed in the dialogue between Orlando and his faithful old servant, Adam, in "As You Like It":

ORLANDO. O good old man! how well in thee appears
The constant service of the antique world,
When service sweat for duty, not for meed!
Thou art not for the fashion of these times,
Where none will sweat but for promotion,
And having that, do choke their service up
Even with the having: it is not so with thee.

. . . .

ADAM. Master, go on, and I will follow thee,
To the last gasp, with truth and loyalty.
From seventeen years till now almost fourscore
Here lived I, but now live here no more.

This old personal relationship is precisely one of the things that cannot endure the present economic revolution. Regret it as we may, it has to go. This, of course, will be unwelcome news to those frank Mediævalists who are even now looking back regretfully to the good old times. One of the strangest of the many strange things in the behavior of the human mind is the way in which this regret for the past mingles, in the same mind, with the general attitude of progressiveness. No one can doubt the broad, social sympathies of the late Maurice Francis Egan and his general progressiveness, and yet he wrote the following: [1]

If simplicity of life consists in the smooth working of every-day affairs without any effort of one, it is impossible to live elegantly and simply without a certain number of servants; and yet the requisite number of servants is virtually an impossibility in any part

[1] *See* "The Fine Art of Simple Living", by Maurice Francis Egan in the *Century Magazine*, June, 1914.

of the United States except among the very rich. We are told over and over again that the absence of a "servant class" in our country is the cause of the anxiety written on nearly every woman's brow when she proposes to entertain guests; but the real cause is the state of mind of the hostess who assumes that her guests demand that she shall be a sacrifice to their expectations. The moment she begins to feel that she must "entertain", her brow becomes dark with depression and her blood feverish with fears; there is no joy in it at all. She has the sole responsibility not only of the amusement and comfort of her guests, but for exciting their admiration or their awe. Her husband hopes that everybody will be comfortable, and that if the carving is not done behind the screen, that the knives will be sharp. If whiskey and soda is good enough for *him*, even the choice of the wines is left to his wife. The whole thing is her affair. If a soup-tureen drops, he looks at *her*, and her furrowed brow can appeal only to heaven, for at that moment she feels that all her women guests are her enemies. The "help" has left her helpless.

The question of servants is no doubt making a huge interrogation point in American life. You cannot have servants without money. Before general instruction became the fashion, when classes were separated by education, servants in all countries were in a measure content to work for what seemed to them and their masters a reasonable sum; but the leveling effect of education has made them free and equal. The servant now uses a place, if he or she is at all clever, to "better" himself or herself, and this "betterment" can be done only by increased wages.

Heretofore a man paid his cook as little as he could. He admitted that a cook was a necessity; but the cook, learning the art of political economy by experience, turned herself into a luxury and said: "There you are! What are you going to do about it?" This is becoming true all over the civilized world; many bad cooks have left Sweden for the United States. Some good ones remain at home and demand high wages. Young ladies, whose chief qualification for uplifting American homes is that they can milk reindeer, are sailing from Norway in the track of their ancestors, glowing with the fire of conquest — the only fire they have yet learned to make. The haughty Irish maid values herself at the price of a case of champagne a month. Why not? If she can cook at all, she is more of a luxury than Veuve Cliquot. What the whole civilized world is beginning to realize is that servants must be classed with truffles, caviar, and pâté de foie gras on the one side, and with soap, fresh air, and steam heat on the other. They are luxuries *and* necessities.

How is life, then, to be led elegantly and simply without servants? That is where practical science ought to come in. Let it settle the question, or forever hold its peace.

No one, who has ever come in contact with the electric mind of Mrs. Cannon, will question her sincere progressiveness; but she is puzzled by the same leveling tendencies that puzzled Mr. Egan, and she even raises the question whether civilization can survive them.[1]

The shortage of domestic servants is a byword in the humorous columns, but for families with frail old people or little children it is not a subject for mirth. Mothers struggle along with burdens too heavy for them to bear, and the integrity of family life suffers. Prohibition has withdrawn from the economic field the last hope of the overburdened American housekeeper, the faithful charwoman, sole support of a drunken husband. That patient drudge is no longer available; she is at the movies with her peers, while the "ladies" wash at home. The high wages the fathers are earning permit their children to remain in school beyond the minimum working age. The resultant reduction in the number of child-workers has become a source of great discomfort to the employers of that type of labor. On the other hand, the pressure on the high schools to care for the enormously increased attendance is making school superintendents old before their time. Grown daughters and wives, in both hand- and brain-occupations, have celebrated the success of the masculine supporter of the family by passing from gainful pursuit into the leisure class. To make confusion worse confounded, the wage-earner himself, by the ex-

[1] *See* "Can Our Civilization Maintain Itself?" by Cornelia James Cannon, in the *Atlantic Monthly* for November, 1920.

penditure of his large wages, has brought additional pressure upon the activities of those who supply his children with amusement, his wife with furs, and his home with victrolas and parlor sets.

Now this matter of servants is precisely one of the things that a balanced economic system will practically eliminate. When cooks and housemaids are about as prosperous as any other class it means that their incomes will be comparable with the incomes of many of those who now employ them, even in this country. This means that the servant-keeping class must necessarily grow still smaller. In fact that tendency is noticeable even now. Since equality of prosperity among occupations does not preclude the possibility of considerable inequality within any given occupation, there will still be a few rich people who can afford to keep servants. The servant-keeping families, however, will be distributed among a large number of occupations. Very rich actors, farmers, authors, plumbers, bankers, butchers, lawyers, auto mechanics, doctors, and many others may still keep servants if they want them. Educated and refined women, unless married to one of these few rich men, will have to do their own housework.

Where a need exists, there is a challenge to the inventive genius of America. It has always met the challenge. One of the acute needs of the time is for ways by which these educated and refined housewives may do their own work without drudgery. Already the need is being met in part, but we are only beginning. One of the rapidly growing businesses of the country is the manufacture of labor-saving devices for the household. In the single item of electric washing machines there is a significant growth. The average monthly sales reached in 1920 the astonishing figure of 47,128 (according to figures of the Department of Commerce). They immediately fell off, with the depression that came at the end of 1920, since which time they have been rising from 24,117 in 1921, to 35,244 in 1922, and to 46,197 in 1923. During 1924 they have risen steadily, month by month, to 56,066 in August and 57,883 in September. The reports are to the effect that there is a similar expansion in the sale of other labor-saving devices for the household, but, unfortunately, definite figures are not available.

If we do not have cheap labor, who will do the other disagreeable work that has to be done? Some have even suggested that we may have to breed morons and imbeciles if we cannot import Mexican peons to do this kind of work. If the work has to be done, there are two better ways than importing semi-slaves, either from Mexico or from heaven. One is to invent machines to do the work, the other is to pay high enough wages to induce men to do it who might be making good wages in any of several other occupations. If we do not want the work done badly enough to undergo either form of expense, it is not so very important. Stinginess, or unwillingness to pay high wages for necessary work, is not a sufficient reason for debasing the population by breeding morons or importing peons.

These hints as to some of the probable results of a balancing of our economic system will suffice to open to the mind of the reader a vast region for speculation. Enchanting as the results may seem, there is not a single item in the program to which any considerable number of Americans object or could object if they tried. Will any reader have the hardihood openly to oppose a system of universal and free education? That is one item in the program of balancing our economic system. Will any considerable number oppose the democratic idea that business is quite as respectable and quite as suitable a field for an educated man as any of the learned professions? Yet that is a means of increasing men where they are scarce and needed to expand our industries and make employment for larger numbers of men, while our system of education is making fewer unskilled laborers to fill the lower positions. Will any except a few hair-brained radicals oppose the development of thrift among all classes? Yet that is a means of increasing capital, decreasing interest rates, and increasing wages. Will any considerable number, except for racial or religious grounds, favor opening the gates to increasing numbers of immigrants? Those who still persist in opposing restriction not only have no economic reason for doing so, but they are so out of touch with the main currents of American thought as to destroy whatever political influence they might otherwise have had. They would better not try to influence voters by saying anything about politics or candidates. The mere fact that a person is known to favor free immigration is enough to make his support a hindrance rather than a help to any candidate or any cause. There are a great many, but they are apparently a minority, who oppose the prohibitory law. A large share of the opposition is from the foreign-born. The mass of the old-timers seems to be for prohibition. Yet this is an item in the balancing-up program. It encourages thrift, and it makes it easier for men to advance to better positions, — men who would otherwise be held in poorly paid positions because of drunkenness. Other items in this program are of the general nature of those just mentioned. There is not one of them that does not, on the whole, enlarge rather than fundamentally restrict the liberty of the individual, and yet every one of these items tends toward greater equality of prosperity among all classes.

The writer hopes that there is not even a hint of pessimism in the tone of this book. This is a glorious country and these are glorious times, but they are growing more glorious. To be alive to-day, in this country, and to remember the years from 1870 to

1920 is to awake from a nightmare. Those were the years when our ideals were all but obscured by the floods of cheap laborers upon whose cheap labor great fortunes were made, and by floods of abuse because we were not instantaneously solving all the social and economic problems these newcomers were inflicting upon us. Those were the years of slums and socialist agitators, of blatant demagogues, and social legislation. We are now emerging into a period when we can give our own ideals a chance to work. Unless all signs fail, we are about to give the world the only great demonstration it has ever had of the practicability of the twin ideals of liberty and equality.

The difficulty which the popular mind has had in holding steadily to both these ideals at the same time, and at all times, is well set forth by De Tocqueville.[1]

"During the period that has elapsed since the Revolution, the passion for liberty has frequently been extinguished again, and again revived. This will long be the case, for it is still inexperienced, ill regulated, easily discouraged, easily frightened away, easily overcome, superficial, and evanescent. Meanwhile, the passion for equality has retained its place at the bottom of the hearts it originally penetrated, and linked with their dearest sentiments. While the one is incessantly changing, now increasing, now

[1] *See* Alexis de Tocqueville, "The Old Régime and the Revolution." Harper and Brothers, New York, 1856. Translated by John Bonner. Pages 252–253, also Preface.

diminishing, now gaining strength, now losing it, according to events, the other has remained uniformly the same, striving for its object with obstinate and often blind ardor, willing to sacrifice everything to gain it, and ready to repay its grant from government by cultivating such habits, ideas, and laws as a despotism may require."

I cannot close this work more fittingly than by quoting again from that distinguished patriot and scholar. I would merely substitute the word American for Frenchman in the second sentence.

"I trust I have written this work without prejudice; but I do not claim to have written dispassionately. It would hardly be decent for a Frenchman to be calm when he speaks of his country, and thinks of the times."

INDEX

INDEX